NAZIK

OCEAN

Novaya
Zemlya

Severnaya
Zemlya

New Siberian
Islands

SWEDEN
FINLAND
ESTONIA
LATVIA
LITHUANIA
BELORUSSIA
POLAND
CZECH
REP.
SLOVAK
REP.
MOL.
UKRAINE
AUSTRIA
HUNGARY
SLOV.
ROMANIA
CRO.
B.-H. YUG.
ITALY
BULGARIA
ALB. MAC.
GREECE

R U S S I A

☐ Moscow

KAZAKHSTAN

MONGOLIA

Kuril
Islands

Peking ☐

NORTH
KOREA

Seoul ☐
SOUTH
KOREA

JAPAN

Tokyo ☐
Osaka

PACIFIC

OCEAN

TUNISIA

TURKEY

GEORGIA
ARMENIA
AZER-
BAIJAN

UZBEKISTAN

KIRGHIZIA

CYPRUS
LEB.
SYRIA
ISRAEL
JORDAN
IRAQ

TURKMENISTAN
TAJIKISTAN

Tehran ☐

IRAN

AFGHANISTAN

CHINA

Shanghai ☐

Ryukyu
Islands

TAIWAN

Hong Kong

LIBYA

Cairo ☐

EGYPT

KUWAIT
BAHRAIN
QATAR
U.A.E.

SAUDI

ARABIA

OMAN

PAKISTAN

Karachi ☐

Delhi ☐

NEPAL
BHUTAN

BANGLA-
DESH
Dacca ☐

Northern
Marianas
(U.S.A.)

NIGER

CHAD

SUDAN

ERITREA
YEMEN

DJIBOUTI

Calcutta ☐

INDIA

Bombay ☐

BURMA

LAOS
VIETNAM

MARSHALL
ISLANDS

ERIA

CAMEROON

CENTRAL
AFRICAN
REPUBLIC

ETHIOPIA

SOMALI REPUBLIC

SRI
LANKA

THAILAND
Bangkok ☐

CAMBODIA

Manila ☐

PHILIPPINES

FEDERATED STATES

OF MICRONESIA

RIAL
EA
GABON
CONGO

CABINDA

UGANDA

ZAIRE

RWANDA
BURUNDI

KENYA

TANZANIA

MALAYSIA

BRUNEI

MALDIVES

SEYCHELLES

SINGAPORE

Sumatra

Borneo

Equator

KIRIBATI

INDONESIA

Jakarta ☐

New
Guinea

PAPUA

NEW GUINEA

SOLOMON
ISLANDS

TUVALU

ANGOLA

ZAMBIA

MALAWI

COMOROS

MADAGASGAR

MAURITIUS

Reunion
(France)

I N D I A N

OCEAN

Cocos Islands
(Australia)

Christmas
Island
(Australia)

VANUATU

FIJI

NAMIBIA

ZIMBABWE

MOZAMBIQUE

BOTSWANA

SWAZILAND

SOUTH

AFRICA

LESOTHO

New
Caledonia
(France)

AUSTRALIA

Prince Edward
Islands
(South Africa)

Crozet
Islands
(France)

Kerguelen
Island
(France)

Tasmania

NEW
ZEALAND

HERN   O C E A N

RCTICA

ALB. = Albania
BEL. = Belgium
B.-H. = Bosnia-Herzegovina
CRO. = Croatia
LEB. = Lebanon
LUX. = Luxembourg
MAC. = Macedonia

MOL. = Moldavia
NETH. = Netherlands
SLOV. = Slovenia
SWITZ. = Switzerland
U.A.E = United Arab Emirates
YUG. = Yugoslavia

![Philip's logo]

FIRST
PICTURE
·ATLAS·

Geoffrey Young

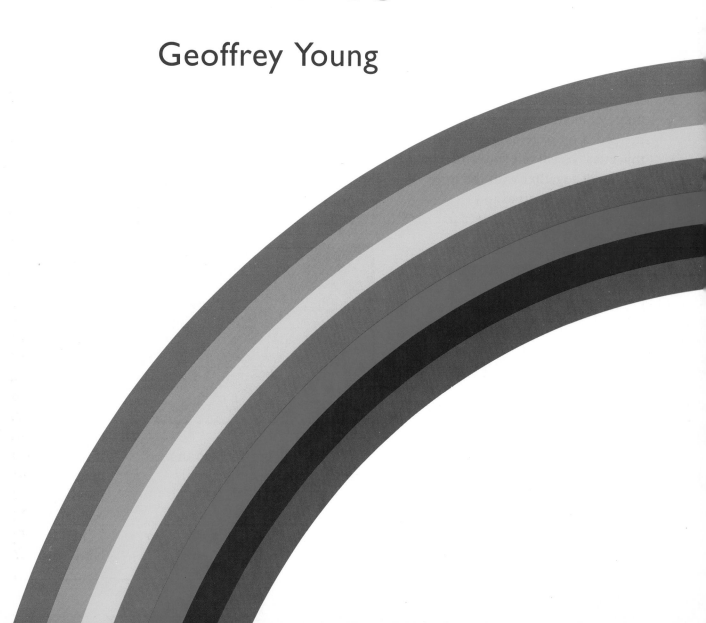

How to use the Atlas

This atlas tells you a lot about many different countries. If you study the maps and look at the pictures, you will find that they are full of things that you did not know.

Mountains, rivers, people's faces from far away, flags, elephants and other animals from around the world – they all appear in this atlas. Here you will learn more about the foreign names and places that you often see on the television news.

What is a camel caravan? And where can you take the longest train journey in the world? These questions and many more are answered here. With this atlas you can travel the world without ever leaving your chair!

Finding places

If you want to find a place on the map, you can look up its name in the Index on page 63 at the end of this atlas. It will tell you which page to look at together with the map square. Here is an example:

Amarillo 55 5 – Amarillo appears in square 5 on map page 55.

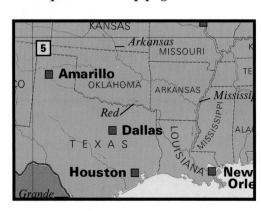

If you know the name of the continent or region where the place is, you can find the correct map from the Contents list. But you may still need to turn to the Index.

About the maps

The coasts of the countries (if they have a coastline) are shown on the maps with a blue line. The frontiers between a country and its neighbours are also shown, but with a red line.

Each country is coloured with a different colour, so that it is easy to tell them apart.

The largest and most important rivers are shown on the maps: they are also shown as a blue line. Rivers usually run to the sea (a few run to large lakes). The small blue arrow shows you the way that the water is flowing.

The names of countries on the maps are written with capital letters, for example INDIA.

Each country's capital city is marked with a red star while other large cities have a red square.

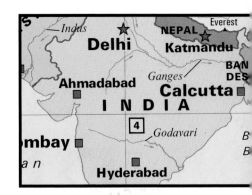

Alongside each map there is a Map Information box. This has a sketch of the Earth showing where the map on that page fits. The top of the maps is the side nearest to the top of the Earth, the North Pole.

In the Map Information boxes there are two lines which are called 'Map Scale'. One line shows kilometres and the other miles. You can use either to help measure the distances between the places on that map. For example, you could write the Map Scale like this:

1 cm equals 160 kilometres
1 inch equals 250 miles

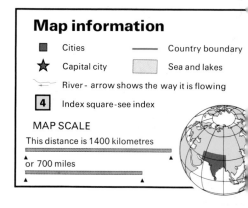

The biggest ranges of mountains are shown on the maps which introduce each continent. The heights of the mountains are measured from the surface of the sea or 'sea level'.

In a few parts of the world the land lies below sea level.

Contents

rst published in Great Britain in 1992
George Philip Limited,
imprint of Reed Consumer Books Limited,
ichelin House, 81 Fulham Road, London SW3 6RB,
d Auckland, Melbourne, Singapore and Toronto
cond edition 1993

artography by Philip's

ext and Maps © 1993 Reed International Books
mited

BN 0 540 05724 X

catalogue record for this book is available from the
itish Library

inted in Hong Kong

Editor: Caroline Rayner
Map Editors: B.M. Willett, Jenny Allen
Designer: Karen Stewart
Picture Research: Karen Gunnell
Flags: Raymond Turvey

Front cover photographs
Bottom left: **Planet Earth Pictures**/Nicholas Tapp
(see p. 49)
Top right: **J. Allan Cash Photolibrary** (see p. 43)

Back cover photographs
Top left: **Zefa Picture Library** (see p. 37)
Top right: **Finnish Tourist Board** (see p. 11)
Bottom left: **The Hutchison Library** (see p. 34)

The Solar System

Relative Sizes of the Planets

Pluto · Neptune · Uranus · Saturn · Jupiter · Sun · Mercury · Venus · Earth · Mars

88 days
225 days
365 days
1.9 years
11.9 years
29.5 years
84 years
165 years
248.5 years

The Sun, the Earth and the Other Planets

The Earth is one of nine planets that move around the Sun. The diagram on the left shows you the names of these planets and the time in days or years that they take to go around the Sun.

The Earth is the third planet in our 'Solar System'. It is quite small compared to some of the other planets. It takes 365 days, or one year, to make one complete circuit of the Sun.

As it circles the Sun, the Earth spins around like a top. When we are facing away from the Sun, it is night-time. When we face the Sun it is daytime. The Earth spins around once a day.

The Earth, the Sun and the Year

Why is it that the weather in Europe and North America is warmest in June and July and coldest in December? The reason is not hard to understand.

The Earth spins once a day as it circles the Sun, but the line round which it spins is not straight up and down. It is tilted, and this means that in summer the North Pole and the northern countries are tilted towards the Sun. The days are then longer and warmer.

In winter, the North Pole is tilted away from the Sun, so that the northern countries are colder and the time that they stay within sight of the Sun is shorter – the days are therefore shorter. Many animals hibernate through the winter.

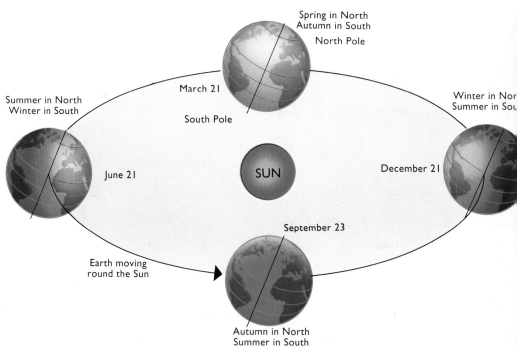

Spring in North
Autumn in South
North Pole

March 21

Summer in North
Winter in South

South Pole

June 21

SUN

December 21

Winter in Nor
Summer in Sou

September 23

Earth moving
round the Sun

Autumn in North
Summer in South

Spring and autumn are halfway times. Plants grow better in the summer, and when it ends many of them allow their leaves to fall off. Autumn is known as the 'fall' in North America.

Because the Earth is tilted in this way, the countries in the south have their seasons at opposite times of the year to the northern countries. In Australia, Christmas Day is in the middle of summer!

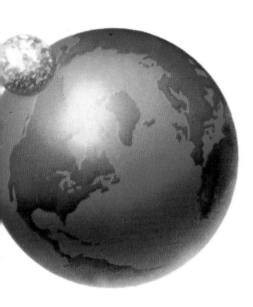

New moon

→ Earth moves round the Sun
--→ Moon moves round the Earth

(New Moon – no image)
2

3

4

Full Moon
5

6

7 8

Old Moon

The Moon

The Moon is made up of rock which is rather similar to the rock found in some parts of the Earth. There is no water and no life on the Moon.

The Moon circles the Earth. We can only see the Moon from the Earth when we can see the side lit up by the Sun. When the Moon is new, for a short time no part can be seen. At Full Moon, we see the whole face lit up by the Sun, as you can see in the pictures above.

The Moon spins on its own axis as it circles the Earth. It does both of these things at the same rate. This means that as it goes round the Earth, it always keeps its far side hidden.

▼ In the far north the Sun does not set in the summer. This means that you can see the Sun at midnight!

The Continents

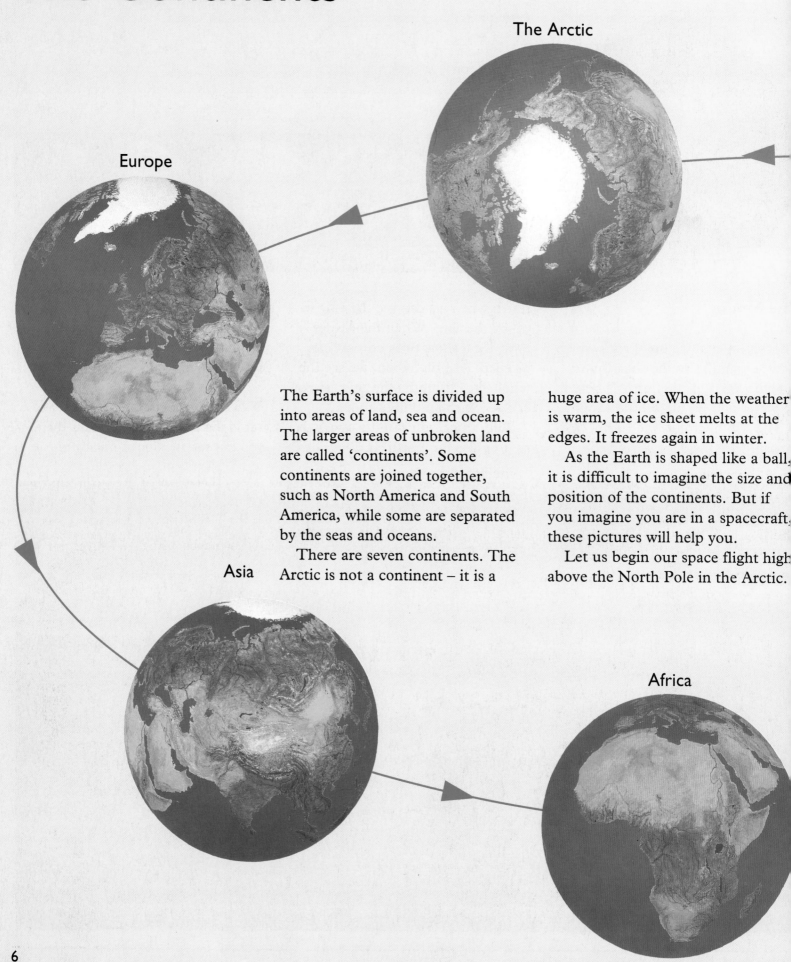

Europe

The Arctic

Asia

Africa

The Earth's surface is divided up into areas of land, sea and ocean. The larger areas of unbroken land are called 'continents'. Some continents are joined together, such as North America and South America, while some are separated by the seas and oceans.

There are seven continents. The Arctic is not a continent – it is a huge area of ice. When the weather is warm, the ice sheet melts at the edges. It freezes again in winter.

As the Earth is shaped like a ball, it is difficult to imagine the size and position of the continents. But if you imagine you are in a spacecraft, these pictures will help you.

Let us begin our space flight high above the North Pole in the Arctic.

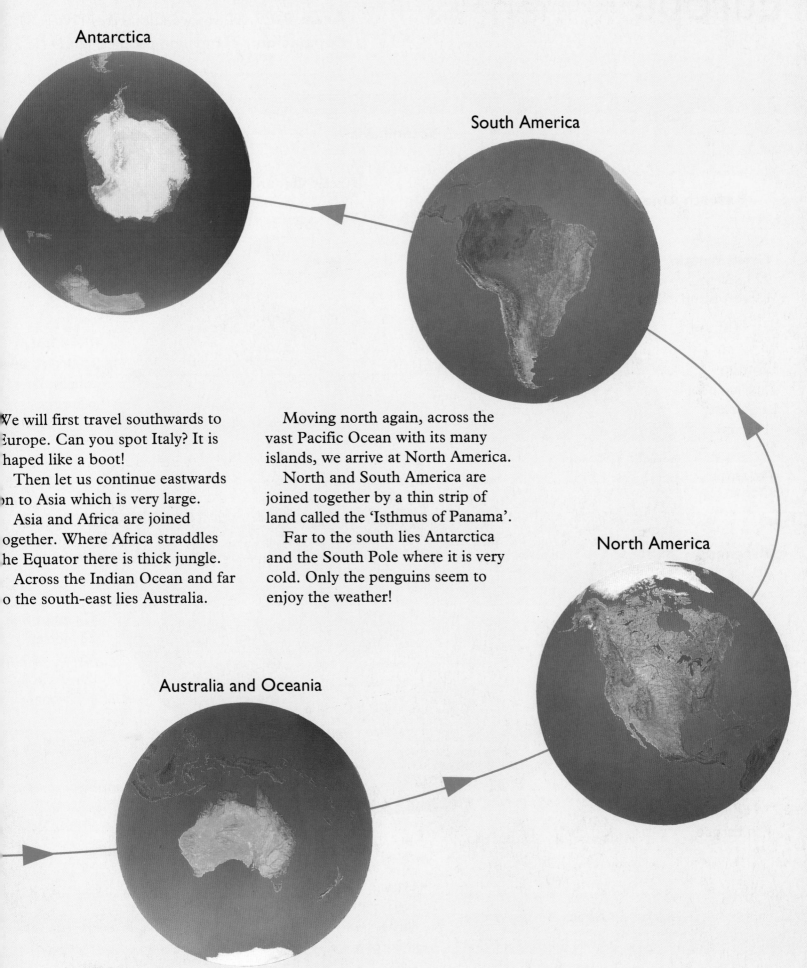

Antarctica

South America

North America

Australia and Oceania

We will first travel southwards to Europe. Can you spot Italy? It is shaped like a boot!

Then let us continue eastwards on to Asia which is very large.

Asia and Africa are joined together. Where Africa straddles the Equator there is thick jungle.

Across the Indian Ocean and far to the south-east lies Australia.

Moving north again, across the vast Pacific Ocean with its many islands, we arrive at North America.

North and South America are joined together by a thin strip of land called the 'Isthmus of Panama'.

Far to the south lies Antarctica and the South Pole where it is very cold. Only the penguins seem to enjoy the weather!

7

Europe

Area: 9,957,000 square kilometres *(World No.6*
Population: 711 million people *(World No.2)*

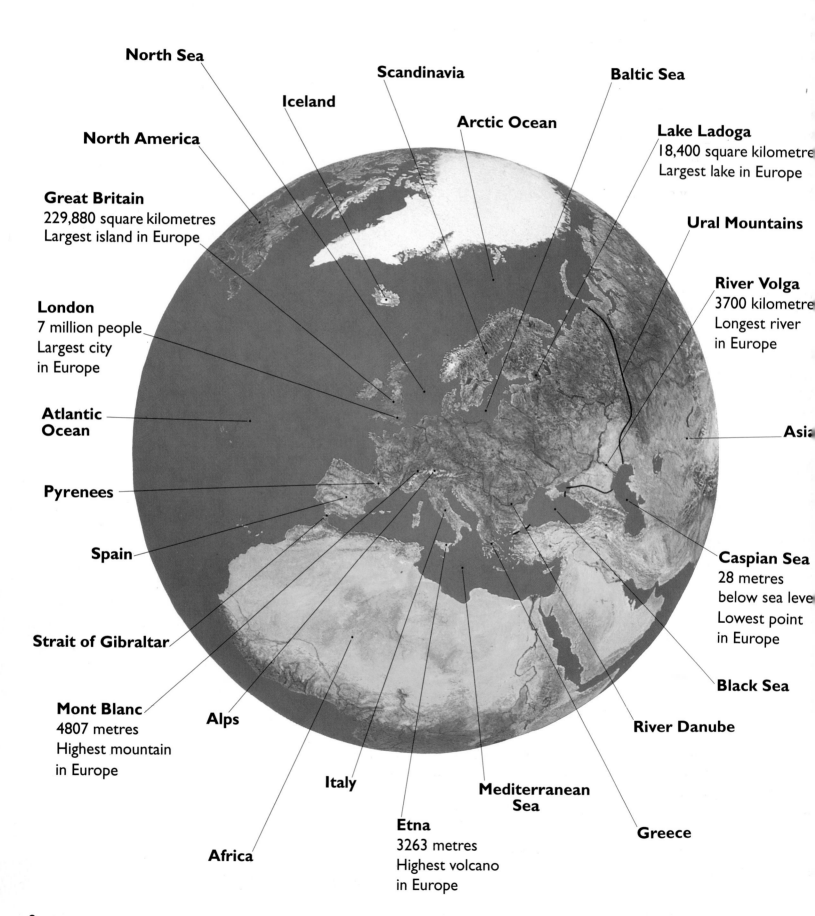

North Sea

Scandinavia

Baltic Sea

Iceland

Arctic Ocean

Lake Ladoga
18,400 square kilometre
Largest lake in Europe

North America

Great Britain
229,880 square kilometres
Largest island in Europe

Ural Mountains

River Volga
3700 kilometre
Longest river
in Europe

London
7 million people
Largest city
in Europe

**Atlantic
Ocean**

Asi:

Pyrenees

Caspian Sea
28 metres
below sea leve
Lowest point
in Europe

Spain

Strait of Gibraltar

Black Sea

Mont Blanc
4807 metres
Highest mountain
in Europe

Alps

River Danube

Italy

**Mediterranean
Sea**

Greece

Etna
3263 metres
Highest volcano
in Europe

Africa

The Pyrenees form a straight wall between Spain and France, while the Alps swing round in a large curve. Mountains are formed when the Earth's rocky crust buckles up, and weathering can carve them into deep towers of rock.

The Earth's crust is still restless in the south of Europe. Earthquakes here are sometimes strong enough to damage buildings, and Mount Vesuvius near Naples in Italy and Mount Etna in Sicily are both active volcanoes.

The lowlands are dotted with farms. North of the Alps the damp weather gives good crops; south of the mountains the Mediterranean climate has much drier summers.

This is a busy and crowded part of the world. Many of the countries are industrialized, with large towns and cities, and modern roads criss-cross the open countryside.

▲ Old castles still proudly stand on guard over the River Rhine, one of the great rivers running from the Alps across Northern Europe. The Rhine has always been an important highway for river traffic, and large barges use it to carry heavy loads across Germany.

Mount Etna on Sicily is still an active volcano as you can see from its plume of smoke. If you visit the mountain, you will see that in some places the forests which grow up its sides have been burnt by the hot molten lava.

The sharp peak of the Matterhorn can be seen in this view of the Swiss Alps in winter. The cable cars take skiers to the high snowfields.

Northern Europe

The northern part of this region is called 'The Land of the Midnight Sun'; in summer it never gets really dark at night because the Sun does not set.

In winter, though, it is a different story. At this time of the year there are only a few hours of daylight. The snow lies deep on the ground and does not melt until May. It is so cold that even the sea in the Gulf of Bothnia sometimes freezes.

The Baltic Sea is a very important shipping route for Scandinavia.

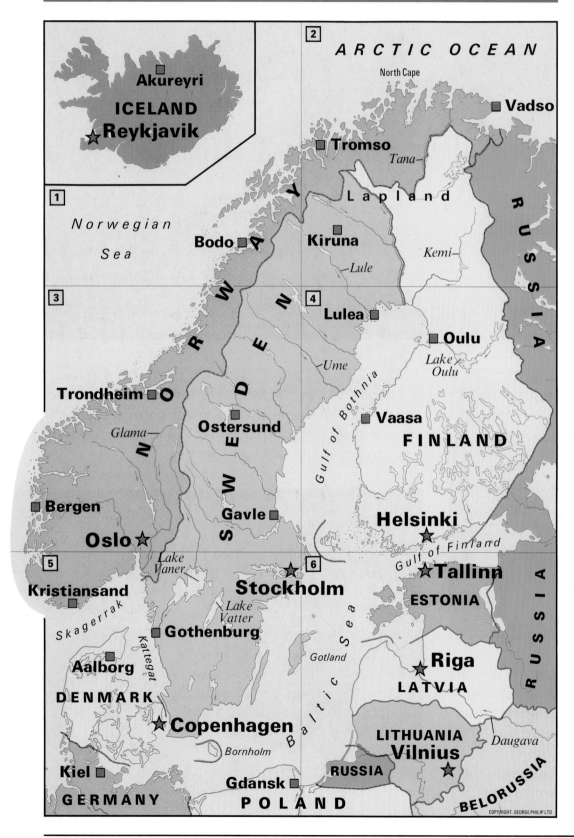

▲ This is the lovely statue of the 'Little Mermaid' in Copenhagen. Hans Christian Andersen wrote about her in his famous fairy-tale.

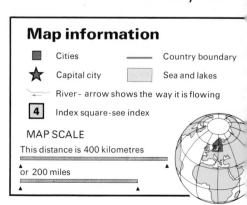

Map information

■ Cities

★ Capital city

〜 River - arrow shows the way it is flowing

4 Index square - see index

――― Country boundary

▨ Sea and lakes

MAP SCALE

This distance is 400 kilometres

or 200 miles

COPYRIGHT. GEORGE PHILIP LTD.

A fjord in Norway. A fjord is a sheltered inlet of the sea which has steep sides and is very deep. Three out of every four Norwegians live within sight of the sea.

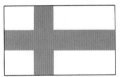

Finland

Denmark

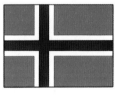

Norway

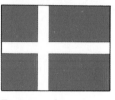

Latvia

▲ This man is a Lapp, one of a race of people who live in Lapland in the north of Finland, Sweden and Norway. His reindeer provide him with milk, meat and skins.

◄ Denmark, Sweden and Norway form a family of countries called 'Scandinavia'. They also have close ties with Iceland and Finland. Their flags are of a similar pattern, though the colours are different. Their languages are also similar, except for Finland. Here they speak Finnish, which is unlike any other European language. Latvia, Lithuania and Estonia are known as the Baltic States.

Most Norwegians live close to the sea, and it is not surprising that they are a seafaring race. Long ago they were called 'Vikings'. They sailed far and wide in open 'longboats' to raid other countries, and some people believe that they even discovered America hundreds of years before Christopher Columbus in 1492.

Sweden and Denmark also have coastlines, and their trade with other countries helped them to become wealthy. Today they spend a lot of money looking after the welfare of their people.

◄ Many people in Scandinavia own boats, but this small harbour in the north of Sweden will be blocked by ice in winter when the sea freezes over.

British Isles

▲ The Yeomen of the Guard are the keepers of the Tower of London, the old fortress of the city. In olden days they were called 'beau-fighters' – meaning sturdy soldiers – a name which in time became 'beefeaters'.

There are mountains in Scotland, the north of England and in Wales. Farms fill the flat countryside and there are many pretty villages with old churches. Cricket, the national game of England, is played on the village greens in summer.

Great Britain was the first industrial nation. Two hundred years ago, the first factory towns were built in the north of England.

A hundred years ago, in the days of Queen Victoria, Great Britain had the greatest empire the world has ever known, so large that the Sun was always shining on a part of it. The countries of the empire are now independent, but 50 are still linked as the 'Commonwealth'.

◄ A peat digger in southern Ireland. The peat will be dried and used on the fire instead of wood. Donkeys are still seen on many farms in the remote parts of Ireland. And most farmers here have a few sheep!

▲ Edinburgh Castle stands on a steep hill overlooking the city. Edinburgh is the old capital of Scotland.

England   Wales

Ireland   Scotland

▲ The Union Jack, the flag of the United Kingdom (which can also be seen in the corner of the Australian flag), is made up of the crosses of England and Scotland, and the red-on-white cross of St Patrick of Ireland. The flag of the Republic of Ireland is a white band of peace between the Catholic (green) and Protestant (orange) religions.

- The longest rivers in the British Isles are the Shannon in Ireland (386 kilometres) and the Severn in England (354 kilometres).
- The tides at the mouth of the Severn are some of the greatest in the world: 12 metres between high and low levels.
- London is one of the world's great cities with 7 million people living there; it is also a very popular city for tourists.

Great Britain is made up of England, Wales, Scotland and the Hebrides and Shetland Islands.

The British Isles once consisted of Great Britain and Ireland, but in 1921 Ireland was divided into Northern Ireland and the Republic of Ireland.

The United Kingdom (UK) consists of England, Scotland, Wales and Northern Ireland, and it has London as its capital.

Liverpool, London, Bristol and Plymouth were four great ports in the days of the British Empire.

Map information

- ■ Cities
- ★ Capital city
- River - arrow shows the way it is flowing
- 4 Index square-see index
- —— Country boundary
- ▢ Sea and lakes

MAP SCALE
This distance is 200 kilometres
or 100 miles

13

The Low Countries

NA3ik

Belgium

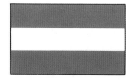
Luxembourg

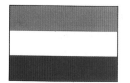
Netherlands

◄ The name 'Netherlands' means 'low-lying lands'. The country with that name is also known as Holland and it language and its people are called Dutch. Belgium and Luxembourg used to be part of the Netherlands but they are now separate countries.

1

2

North Sea

Frisian Islands

Waddenzee

Groningen

Den Helder ■

IJssel Lake

Being reclaimed

3

Haarlem ■

4 ☆ Amsterdam

NETHERLANDS

The Hague ☆

■ Utrecht

Hook of Holland ■

Lek

Waal

Rotterdam ■

Nijmegen ■

Rhine

Maas

Walcheren

Eindhoven ■

Essen ■

Ostend ■

■ Antwerp

Dusseldorf ■

Bruges ■

■ Ghent

B E L G I U M

G E R M A N Y

5

☆

Brussels

6

Maastricht ■

Lille ■

Liege ■

Bonn ■

Charleroi ■

Meuse

■ Amiens

■ St.-Quentin

Moselle

LUXEMBOURG

F R A N C E

Luxembourg ☆

There are two capital cities in the Netherlands
Amsterdam is the capital city and the government is at The Hague.

COPYRIGHT, GEORGE PHILIP LTD.

▲ Lace making was once a very important industry in Belgium and some lace is still made. The patterns of this woman's blouse and cap have remained unchanged for 300 years.

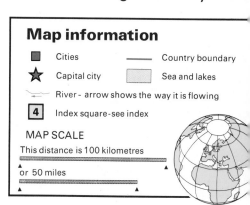

Map information

■ Cities ——— Country boundary

☆ Capital city ▒ Sea and lakes

∿ River - arrow shows the way it is flowing

4 Index square-see index

MAP SCALE

This distance is 100 kilometres

or 50 miles

There it crosses the Netherlands, the great River Rhine is given Dutch names. You can see that it divides into branches on its way to the sea, which is a clue that the land here is very flat. In fact, more than half of the Netherlands is below sea level.

The land has been won from the sea with the help of pumps and drainage canals; and you will see that some town names end in the word 'dam', such as Rotter*dam*.

The canals are also used by barges. In the towns, old barges are sometimes used as floating homes.

Round cheeses for sale in a Dutch town. Open markets like this are often seen in Europe. The wooden 'sledge' is carried by two men and is used instead of a barrow with wheels to transport the cheeses.

▲ Many Dutch farmers grow flowers for sale. Nowadays the fields are drained dry with electric pumps, but old wind pumps looking like windmills can still be seen.

◄ A canal in the town of Bruges in Belgium, lined with old houses which once belonged to merchants. Their barges could be moored on the canal below.

In days gone by, the people of the Netherlands went in search of the world's wealth and had a great empire. Rotterdam is still the world's largest port, used by supertankers carrying oil for the whole of Europe.

A modern name for these three countries is 'Benelux' – can you guess why? The three countries play an important role in world affairs. The headquarters of the European Community are in *Be*lgium, the International Courts of Justice are in the *Ne*therlands, and many businesses are based in *Lux*embourg.

Germany and Austria

■ Every year 14 million people visit Austria for a holiday – twice as many people as live there. Many go there to ski in winter.

▶ Fireworks light up the sky over the Brandenburg Gate in Berlin. The fireworks celebrate the day in 1990 when West and East Germany were reunited as one country after being divided for 45 years.

In the north, Germany stretches to the Baltic Sea and the North Sea. Hamburg is an important port for ships from all over the world. Here the country is flat and well farmed, with large fields of wheat and other crops. It is hillier in the south and there are many forests.

Germany is a busy modern nation with a lot of different industries. It was divided into two separate parts, a democratic 'West' and communist 'East', at the end of World War II, and the capital cities were Bonn and Berlin.

But in 1990, the two countries were reunited again. Can you tell from the map which city is now the capital of Germany?

Map information

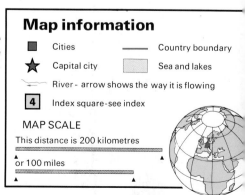

■ Cities
★ Capital city

—— Country boundary

Sea and lakes

River - arrow shows the way it is flowing

4 Index square-see index

MAP SCALE

This distance is 200 kilometres

or 100 miles

When the hour strikes, the figures of the famous 'Glockenspiel' on the Town Hall in Munich hammer out a tune and dance.

The steep grassy meadows called 'alps' give these mountains their name. Beyond this small Austrian village stands the snow-covered mountain Grossglockner.

Germany

Austria

▲ Lippizaner horses step out in a dance in the indoor riding school in Vienna. Sadly, this splendid building, dating back to the Austro-Hungarian Empire, was damaged by fire in 1992.

◄ The colour and design of the German flag was accepted by East Germany when the two countries were reunited. The Austrian flag dates from 1918.

The high Alps cross Austria and it is a mountainous country. The people speak German – but with a different accent! Austria and Hungary once formed a great empire, with Vienna as its capital. Palaces and other fine buildings remain from those years.

Liechtenstein is a small independent country. It is also one of the richest countries in the world.

Eastern Europe

▲ Poland is a busy country with farms, mines, factories and towns, but there are also great forests where wolves still roam. This is part of the Tatra National Park.

▶ A quaint street in Prague, the capital of the Czech Republic. You can see that there is not much traffic! A long time ago, Good King Wenceslas of the Christmas carol ruled here.

■ Russia is a powerful modern nation. Moscow has the busiest metro (underground) system in the world, carrying 7 million passengers every day.

■ Czechoslovakia split into two republics in January 1993: the Czech Republic and the Slovak Republic. The Czech President, Vaclav Havel, is also a playwright.

In olden days the empire of the Tsars, who were the emperors of Russia, spread from the Baltic Sea to the Pacific Ocean. A revolution in 1917 overthrew them and Russia

◀ The colourful 'onion' domes of St Basil's Cathedral, in the Kremlin, Moscow. The Kremlin was the Tsar's palace but it is now being used by the government as offices.

became communist. It then seized other countries on its borders, and with them created the Union of Soviet Socialist Republics (USSR).

The USSR was often called 'Russia'. Its flag was red, with a gold hammer and sickle. This flag also flew in Poland and other countries in Eastern Europe. The USSR is now broken up, and these 'Eastern Bloc' countries are independent.

Ukraine   Poland

▲ Poland used to be one of the 'Eastern Bloc' countries controlled by the communist Soviet Union, but it is now free. The Ukraine was once part of the USSR but is now a separate country using its old flag.

Poland is an old country, but its borders are not protected by mountains and it has often been invaded. Hungary is also old, and until World War I was part of the large Austro-Hungarian Empire. Both of these countries belonged to the 'Eastern Bloc', but now that the Soviet Union has broken up they are making new links with Germany and other free Western countries.

▲ A castle in the Crimea, on a cliff overlooking the Black Sea. The Crimea separates the Sea of Azov from the Black Sea – which (as you can see) is not really black!

■ Russian is a 'Slav' language and different in many ways to other European languages. It shares letters with English, but they are pronounced differently. The English letters C, P, H and B are pronounced 'S', 'R', 'N' and 'V'.

Map information

■ Cities
★ Capital city
River - arrow shows the way it is flowing
4 Index square-see index

Country boundary
Sea and lakes

MAP SCALE
This distance is 800 kilometres
or 400 miles

France

France is crossed by great rivers which flow to two different seas – the Atlantic and the Mediterranean. It shares frontiers with five other countries, and its frontiers with Switzerland and Italy are very mountainous. Europe's highest mountain, Mont Blanc (4807 metres), is here. In the south, Provence has sunny beaches which attract holidaymakers. The island of Corsica also belongs to France.

- French farmers make over 500 different kinds of cheese.
- Football and bicycle racing are the two favourite sports.

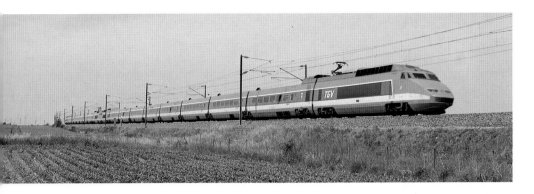

The TGV or Train de Grand Vitesse (meaning 'Very Fast Train') is the world's fastest passenger train. It travels at 270 kilometres per hour.

France is a modern nation with the best railways and roads in Europe, but the French countryside is still peaceful. The French are proud of their elegant language and also like to eat well. France is famous for its excellent food and wine.

Although it took place a long time ago, many good things in French life are the result of the French Revolution. In 1789 the King and his decadent court were overthrown, and their wealth was seized by the ordinary people. The revolutionaries tried to create a fairer society, with new laws and new kinds of schools for children.

▲ The Château of Saumur overlooks the River Loire. Many aristocrats in the 18th century had homes like this on the banks of the Loire, as it was not too far away from Paris.

▲ The Eiffel Tower in Paris is 320 metres high. It was built in 1889 and is a very popular tourist attraction.

Map information

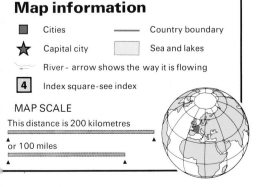

■ Cities	——	Country boundary
★ Capital city		Sea and lakes
River - arrow shows the way it is flowing		
4 Index square-see index		

MAP SCALE

This distance is 200 kilometres

or 100 miles

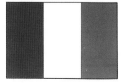

France

▲ Sunflowers in the countryside near Toulouse, their faces to the sun. They are mainly grown to make sunflower oil.

◄ The Tricolore, the three-coloured flag of France, was first flown during the French Revolution in 1789.

Spain and Portugal

1 Cape Finisterre

La Coruna

Gijon
2 Bay of Biscay
Santander
Bilbao   San Sebastian
Bayonne
3 Toulouse
F R A N C E
Perpignan
ANDORRA

Minho
Vigo
Leon
Burgos

Valladolid
Zaragoza   Ebro
Barcelona   Costa Brava

Oporto
4 Douro

Salamanca
5 Segovia
6

Coimbra

P O R T U G A L

Madrid ☆
S P A I N
Castellon

Toledo
Tagus
Valencia

☆ Lisbon   Badajoz
Albacete   Jucar

Balearic Island   Minorca
Majorca
Palma
Ibiza

Guadiana

7
Alicante
9

Murcia

Cordoba
Guadalquivir
Cartagena

Lagos
Cape St Vincent
Seville
A n d a l u c i a
Granada

Gulf of Cadiz
Malaga
Algiers

Cadiz
Costa   del   Sol
Almeria

M e d i t e r r a n e a n   Sea

Gibraltar
(U.K.)
Strait of Gibraltar   Ceuta
(Sp.)
MOROCCO
A L G E R I A

8

○ Melilla, a town in North Africa, and the Canary Islands are parts of Spain.

COPYRIGHT: GEORGE PHILIP LTD.

Map information

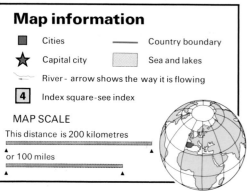

■ Cities

★ Capital city

⤙ River - arrow shows the way it is flowing

4 Index square-see index

— Country boundary

▨ Sea and lakes

MAP SCALE

This distance is 200 kilometres

or 100 miles

■ Nearly 39 million Spaniards live in Spain, but every summer they are joined by 30 million tourists from all over Europe who come for a sunny holiday. The beaches of the Costa Brava and the Costa del Sol are very popular.

■ 10 million holidaymakers also join the 10 million people who live in Portugal.

■ The 'Rock' of Gibraltar is still a British colony; 30,000 people live there, speaking English and Spanish.

The Moors left Spain a legacy of beautiful buildings. This fine fountain is in the Moorish Alhambra Palace in Granada, a town in Andalucia in the south of the country.

▲ This is the cathedral of Segovia, an old city in the centre of Spain. The cathedral was built at a time when Spain's empire made it the richest country in the world. Many Spanish cities have magnificent cathedrals like this and even the villages have grand churches. The Roman Catholic religion still plays an important part in daily life.

Africa nearly meets Europe at the south of Spain. The Moors, who were Arabs from North Africa, invaded Spain and held it for many centuries. Moorish music has since become the thrilling flamenco music that we can hear in Spain today.

Both Spain and Portugal had large empires in Central and South America, and the countries there still speak Spanish or Portuguese. In fact, it was a Spanish expedition which first discovered America in 1492 with Christopher Columbus.

Although many tourists now visit Spain and Portugal, there are still quiet villages behind the busy beaches where goats and donkeys are a familiar sight. However, even in remote villages, life for the people is becoming fairer and more modern.

Spain

Portugal

▲ The distant empires are lost, but the Spanish flag still flies over the Balearic Islands (Majorca, Minorca and Ibiza) and the Canary Islands. Madeira and the Azores are still Portuguese.

◀ Mending the fishing nets on a Portuguese beach. A restful scene, but the fishermen will spend the night far out on the dark ocean in these small boats.

Switzerland and Italy

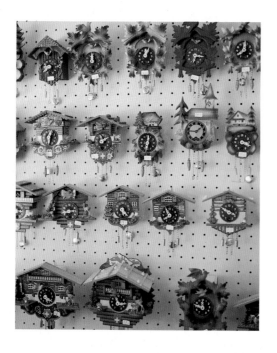

- The Italian language is spoken throughout Italy. But there is no Swiss language – the people of Switzerland speak either German, French or Italian.
- Switzerland is a neutral country.

◀ The skilled craftsmen of Switzerland have made cuckoo clocks for centuries. On the hour, the bird will pop out and call once for each hour to tell you the time. The Swiss are also famous for their watchmaking – and chocolate!

Switzerland

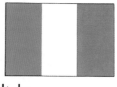

Italy

Both Switzerland and northern Italy are mountainous with many large lakes. Most of the 'boot' of Italy is also hilly, especially in the south, where the weather is very warm for most of the year. Mount Vesuvius near Naples and Mount Etna on Sicily are active volcanoes and they are often seen smoking

Italy has had a busy history. At the time of Christ, Rome was the head of a great empire stretching from Britain to Asia. During the 'Renaissance' (which means 'rebirth') 500 years ago, many splendid churches and palaces were built which can still be seen today.

Italy includes Sicily and Sardinia However, San Marino and the Vatican City in Rome remain independent states. The Vatican is the headquarters of the Pope and the Roman Catholic religion.

Although many people in the Italian countryside live simply, Italy is now an advanced nation, famous for its modern design in clothes, cars and other things.

▲ The symbol for the International Red Cross comes from the Swiss flag. The colours of the Italian flag date from the time of Napoleon in 1796.

▲ A farmstead in the Italian countryside of Tuscany, surrounded by neat rows of grapevines.

▶ The Colosseum in Rome once seated 500,000 people, but now after nearly 2000 years it is in ruins.

1

Basle
Zurich
★ **Bern**
SWITZERLAND
Geneva

Lake Constance

Inn

2 GERMANY

Salzburg

Innsbruck

LIECHTENSTEIN

AUSTRIA

Klagenfurt

Lake Geneva
Rhône
Lugano
Milan
Turin

Bolzano

Lake Garda

Venice

Ljubljana ★

SLOVENIA

Trieste

CROATIA

Po

Genoa

Bologna

3 Nice
MONACO

Gulf of Genoa

Pisa

4 Florence

Tuscany

—SAN MARINO

5 *Adriatic Sea*

BOSNIA-HERZEGOVINA

Split

CROATIA

Dubrovnik

YUGOSLAVIA

Elba

Corsica
(France)

Ajaccio

Perugia

Tiber

Pescara

VATICAN CITY ★ **Rome**

Sassari

Sardinia
(Italy)

6

Naples
▲ *Mount Vesuvius*

Bari

ALBANIA

Brindisi

Strait of Otranto

7

8

Gulf of Taranto

Cagliari

Tyrrhenian   Sea

Ionian   Sea

Lipari Islands

Palermo

Messina

Mediterranean

Egadi Islands

Mount Etna ▲

Strait of Messina

Sicily

Catania

Tunis
★
TUNISIA

Pantelleria

Sea

COPYRIGHT. GEORGE PHILIP LTD.

■ Italy is a crowded country with 57 million people, but there are only 6 million in Switzerland.

Map information

■ Cities
★ Capital city

—— Country boundary
☐ Sea and lakes

⌇ River - arrow shows the way it is flowing

4 Index square-see index

MAP SCALE

This distance is 200 kilometres

or 100 miles

South-east Europe

■ One of the highest mountains in this region is Mount Olympus. It is 2917 metres high.
■ The River Danube now passes eight countries on its way from Germany to the Black Sea.

◀ Farm workers in Albania are seen here sorting green apples. Albania is one of the poorest countries in this region and most Albanian people work on the land.

▼ This part of the world is known as 'The Balkans'. It has always been a restless region, and the frontiers of the countries have often changed as a result of wars and invasions. Except for Greece, these countries were at one time controlled by the Soviet Union but are now independent.

Romania

Hungary

Albania

Greece

Map information

■	Cities	—	Country boundary
☆	Capital city		Sea and lakes
	River - arrow shows the way it is flowing		
4	Index square - see index		

MAP SCALE
This distance is 400 kilometres

or 200 miles

CZECH REPUBLIC
SLOVAK REPUBLIC
Kosice
UKRAINE
UKRAINE
Vienna
Bratislava
Iasi
Kishinev
AUSTRIA
MOLDAVIA
Budapest
HUNGARY
Cluj
Prut
Ljubljana
Drava
ROMANIA
SLOVENIA
Zagreb
Tisza
Timisoara
CROATIA
Sava
Iron Gates
Bucharest
BOSNIA-HERZEGOVINA
YUGOSLAVIA
Belgrade
Danube
Split
Sarajevo
Varna
Morava
BULGARIA
Black Sea
Dubrovnik
Skopje
Sofia
ITALY
Tirane
MACEDONIA
Plovdiv
Istanbul
Bari
ALBANIA
Naples
Thessaloniki
Mount Olympus
TURKEY
Tyrrhenian Sea
Aegean Sea
Izmir
GREECE
Ionian Sea
Athens
Ionian Islands
Sicily
Catania
Dodecanese
Rhodes
Iraklion
MALTA
Valletta
Mediterranean Sea
Crete

COPYRIGHT GEORGE PHILIP L

There are many mountains in this region, but the Danube, the largest river, runs across wide plains between the mountain ranges. It crosses the mountains at a famous gorge called 'The Iron Gates'.

Apart from violent clashes between the countries themselves, long ago in history they were also invaded by Turkey and by other Muslim armies from the east. Buildings from these times remain in some places.

Although it had no great empire of its own, Greece was once the cradle of European civilization. It was in Greece, 2500 years ago, that science and mathematics began to be studied properly for the first time.

▲ This lovely church sits on an island in the middle of Lake Bled in Slovenia. Up until 1992 Slovenia was part of Yugoslavia – it is now an independent country along with Croatia.

◄ A Romanian farmer makes his way home from the fields after a day's work. Although Romania has built many factories, most people still work on the land and are very poor. Without the money to buy tractors, oxen are often used to pull the plough.

■ Albania is a 'closed' country and very difficult for strangers to visit.
■ Greece and its islands have millions of tourists each year.
■ Athens is one of the busiest airports in Europe.

A catch of octopus hangs drying in the sunshine in Crete, the largest of the Greek islands. In the summer these islands are busy with many holidaymakers, but fishing and the old ways of life still continue.

Asia NAZiK

Area : 44,500,000 square kilometres *(World No.*
Population : 3,183 million people *(World No.1)*

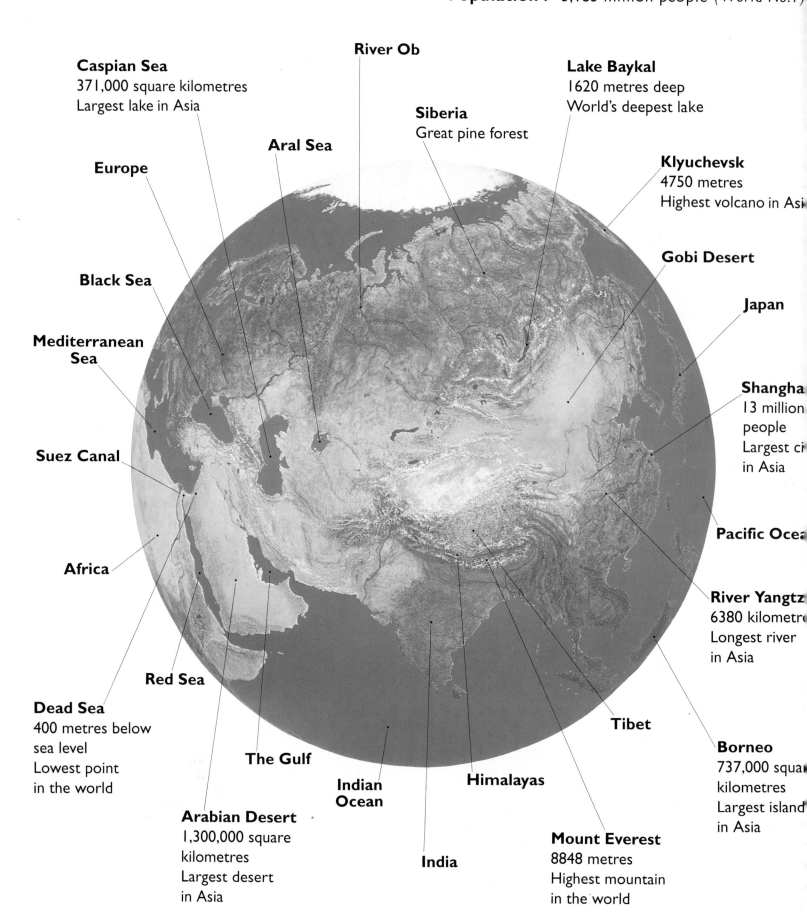

Caspian Sea
371,000 square kilometres
Largest lake in Asia

River Ob

Lake Baykal
1620 metres deep
World's deepest lake

Siberia
Great pine forest

Aral Sea

Klyuchevsk
4750 metres
Highest volcano in Asi

Europe

Gobi Desert

Black Sea

Japan

**Mediterranean
Sea**

Shangha
13 million
people
Largest ci
in Asia

Suez Canal

Pacific Ocea

Africa

River Yangtz
6380 kilometre
Longest river
in Asia

Red Sea

Tibet

Dead Sea
400 metres below
sea level
Lowest point
in the world

Borneo
737,000 squa
kilometres
Largest island
in Asia

The Gulf

**Indian
Ocean**

Himalayas

Arabian Desert
1,300,000 square
kilometres
Largest desert
in Asia

India

Mount Everest
8848 metres
Highest mountain
in the world

▲ An oasis in the Gobi Desert in Mongolia. Much of this desert is very high above sea level and temperatures can reach 45°C in summer but fall to − 40°C in winter. The sharp edges of the dunes show that the desert sand is loose and windblown, but other parts are rockier. There are few roads here!

Mount Everest is the highest mountain in the world t 8848 metres. It is one of the many peaks in the limalayas, which form the world's mightiest mountain ange. The name Himalaya means 'home of the snows'.

▼ Fields have been carved like steps out of these hills in the Philippines, with banks to trap the rain so that rice can be grown in them. Rice is a main crop in large parts of Asia, but it needs plenty of water.

sia extends from Europe to the 'acific, but everything is bigger. ts mountain ranges are larger and igher, and its rivers are longer. Its ablelands and deserts are vast and lmost empty. Even the weather is nore extreme than it is in Europe – uch hotter when it is hot, and ery much colder when it is cold. he pine forests of Siberia are even arger than the Amazon jungle.

Asia spreads south past the quator, and then breaks up into housands of islands. Here the veather is tropical and wet and the and is much more populated. Most eople in Asia live by farming in ome way.

Northern Asia

Map labels:
ARCTIC OCEAN
Svalbard (Norway)
Wrangel Island
Franz Josef Land
New Siberian Islands
Severnaya Zemlya
Bering Sea
Novaya Zemlya
North Cape
Kamchat Peninsu
UNITED KINGDOM
Oslo NORWAY
SWEDEN
Stockholm
Murmansk
FINLAND
Riga Tallinn ESTONIA
LITHUANIA LATVIA
Vilnius
Archangel
Minsk BELORUSSIA
UKRAINE
Kiev Moscow
MOLDAVIA
Kishinev
Volga
Lena
Yakutsk
Sea of Okhotsk
S i b e r i a
Yenisey
Sakhalin
R U S S I A
Yekaterinburg
Ob
Samara
Krasnodar
Irtysh
Novosibirsk
Krasnoyarsk
Ural
Lake Baykal
Amur
GEORGIA
Caspian Sea
KAZAKHSTAN
Angara
Irkutsk
Chita
Harbin
Vladivostok
Tbilisi
ARMENIA
Yerevan
AZERBAIJAN
Aral Sea
Syr
Lake Balkhash
Sea of Japan
Toky
Baku
UZBEKISTAN
NORTH KOREA
JAPA
Amu
Ulan Bator MONGOLIA
Pyongyang SOUTH KOREA
Tehran
TURKMENISTAN
Tashkent
Alma-Ata
KIRGHIZIA
Bishkek
Urumchi
Peking (Beijing)
Seoul
Ashkhabad
TAJIKISTAN
Dushanbe
Hwang Ho
Yellow Sea
Kuril Islands
IRAQ
IRAN
C H I N A
AFGHANISTAN
COPYRIGHT. GEORGE PHILIP

◀ A woman from Mongolia with a warm cap made of young soft goatskin. Mongolia is a harsh country with empty deserts and frozen ground. Much of the land is more than 1500 metres above sea level.

Map information

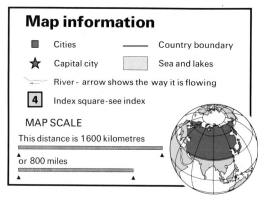

▪ Cities
★ Capital city
— Country boundary
▢ Sea and lakes
⤳ River - arrow shows the way it is flowing
4 Index square-see index

MAP SCALE
This distance is 1600 kilometres
or 800 miles

Russia is a vast country, nearly as large as Canada and the USA added together. In the eastern part of Russia is the region known as 'Siberia'.

The north of Siberia is open countryside without trees. It is frozen for most of the year. Furthe south there is a vast fir forest. Today there are coal and other mines in Siberia.

The countries to the south of Siberia can also have harsh weathe but canals have been dug in recent years to bring water. Tea, sugar and other crops are now grown.

Two market women wait for customers in Tashkent, the capital city of Uzbekistan. Uzbekistan is mainly made up of deserts and plains. A long time ago, fierce nomadic tribes from countries such as this invaded far to the west, even as far as Europe. Today 20 million people live in Uzbekistan.

After the Revolution in 1917, Russia enlarged its empire and created the Soviet Union, uniting many Asian countries under the communist Red Flag with its golden hammer and sickle. These countries are now free, and some now fly their old flags again, including Russia itself. The crescent is a symbol of the Muslim religion which is strong in many of these countries.

Russia

Mongolia

Uzbekistan

Azerbaijan

▲ A herdsman in Kazakhstan. This country is almost as large as India but is mainly made up of dry, bleak open plains like the one in the picture. The people are very skilled horsemen and many of them still live their traditional nomadic way of life, following their sheep as they feed across the unfenced plains.

These camels of Northern Asia are a different breed from the 'Arabian' camels of North Africa. Here in Mongolia they pull carts as well as being used for carrying heavy back-packs. In olden days, camel 'caravans' used to travel long distances across Asia, laden with silk and spices from China.

■ It takes seven days to travel from Moscow to Vladivostok on the Trans-Siberian Railway, which is the world's longest railway (trans means 'across'). This railway is 9438 kilometres long and has 97 stops.
■ Lake Baykal in Russia has the largest volume of fresh water in the world. It holds as much water as all the Great Lakes of North America put together.

China, Japan and Eastern Asia

▶ China is a communist country but Taiwan is a refuge for Chinese people who are anti-communist. Japan and South Korea have become industrial nations, and now sell their goods all over the world.

▼ The Great Wall of China stretches for 3460 kilometres. It was built to protect China against invaders from the north. A wonder of the world!

China

Taiwan

South Korea

Japan

▼ Two charming young girls have dressed in the kimonos of olden days to pose for their photograph on a bridge amongst the springtime cherry blossom in a garden near Tokyo, the capital of Japan.

▲ Monks blow trumpets during a ceremony in their temple in Lhasa, the capital of Tibet. For centuries Tibet was one of the most remote countries in the world, visited by very few outsiders.

This part of the world has vast dry deserts and remote, secret empty lands hidden by high mountains, but it also has very fertile plains and many islands.

Where people are able to live, they live in large numbers. One fifth of all the people alive in the world today are Chinese.

Ancient languages are spoken here, and different alphabets are used in writing. The name now written as 'Beijing' used to be written as 'Peking'.

There are great contrasts here. Tibet remains cut off from the rest of the world. But Japan and South Korea are quite the opposite.

Their people have learnt new skills and their factories make computers and other modern 'silicon chip' machines which are sold all over the world.

China is also quickly becoming more modern in this way. But old traditions survive everywhere, and visitors are still greeted with smiles.

Map information

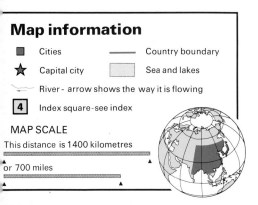

■	Cities	▬	Country boundary
★	Capital city	▬	Sea and lakes
			River - arrow shows the way it is flowing
4	Index square - see index		

MAP SCALE

This distance is 1400 kilometres

or 700 miles

- ■ Remote Tibet is 5000 metres above sea level.
- ■ More than 1 billion people live in China.

▲ Hong Kong is a British colony. It is a centre for worldwide banking and trade. In 1997 it will become Chinese, like the old-fashioned 'junk' seen here sailing in front of the modern skyscrapers.

South-east Asia

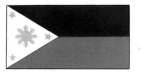

Philippines   Thailand

▲ Thailand welcomes thousands of visitors each year. The blue stripe was added to its flag after World War I. The three small stars in the flag of the Philippines represent its three main island groups.

Many different races and tribes live side by side in these colourful countries, making it a restless part of the world. Even the rocks below ground seem restless, for there are frequent earthquakes.

You can see from the map that many of the countries in this region are made up of lots of islands. Indonesia has about 13,000 islands and is the world's largest island chain.

There are still many areas covered with dense jungle filled with exotic animals and birds.

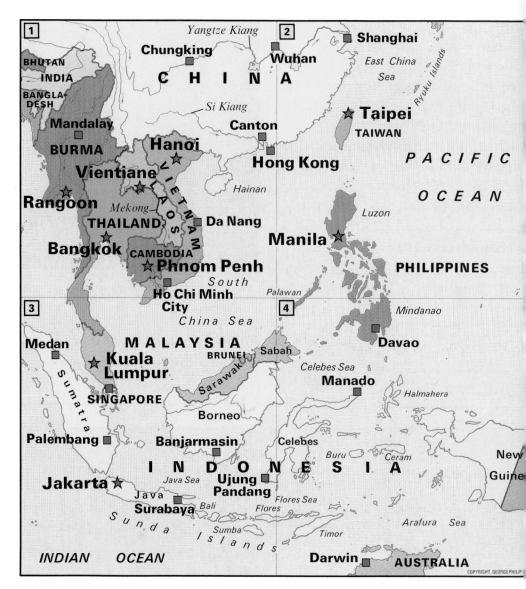

COPYRIGHT. GEORGE PHILIP

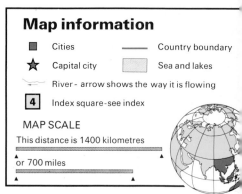

Map information

■ Cities   —— Country boundary

★ Capital city   Sea and lakes

～ River - arrow shows the way it is flowing

4 Index square - see index

MAP SCALE

This distance is 1400 kilometres

or 700 miles

◀ These are some of the Buddhist temples in the 'City of a Thousand Temples' at Pagan in Burma. In Rangoon there is the world's largest statue of Buddha, lying on its side and measuring 78 metres long.

The rice harvest in Bali. Rice is the main food of the people. Heavy rains and hot sun make this region one of the best rice gardens in the whole world.

► A mother and her family, members of a hill tribe in Thailand. Their clothes are elaborately and colourfully decorated, as you can see.

It is hot and wet here for most of the year, with monsoon rains and many tropical thunderstorms. Everybody eats rice, usually made tastier with pieces of dried fish or spiced meat and vegetables. Every country is proud of its own style of cooking.

Until they became independent, many of the countries here were European colonies. There was an important trade in spices and also rubber. Rubber is the dried sap collected from the rubber tree.

■ Singapore holds the record as the most crowded country in the world. In area, it is one of the smallest.

◄ This is a floating market in Thailand where fruit and vegetables are being sold. Many people live alongside the water here, often in houseboats.

South Asia

Rivers rise in mountains and flow through valleys and across plains. The rivers marked on the map below tell you where the mountains lie. India's northern border is mountainous and empty of people, but the wide plains crossed by the Indus and Ganges rivers are very crowded indeed.

Map information

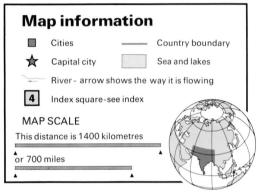

- ▪ Cities
- ★ Capital city
- ━━━ Country boundary
- ▨ Sea and lakes
- 〜 River - arrow shows the way it is flowing
- 4 Index square-see index

MAP SCALE

This distance is 1400 kilometres

or 700 miles

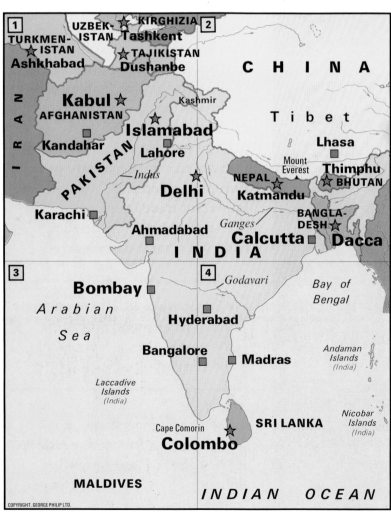

COPYRIGHT. GEORGE PHILIP LTD.

Pakistan

India

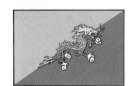

Bhutan

▲ In these colourful countries, old festivals and customs linger on in the modern world. Here a snake charmer teases a poisonous cobra with the movement of his pipe. The snake rears up and sways to the movement of the pipe – not its sound, which it cannot hear.

◀ The colours of flags often have a meaning. Here they show different religions: the red in the Indian flag means 'Hindu', the green 'Muslim'. India also has Sikhs and Buddhists. Pakistan and Bangladesh are both Muslim. Bhutan is also known as the 'Land of the Dragon'.

- ▪ In this region live a quarter of the people alive in the world today.
- ▪ 800 million people live in India.
- ▪ Mount Everest on the Nepal border is the highest mountain in the world at 8848 metres.

Rice is the favourite food of most of the people in this crowded part of the world, and rice needs plenty of water. For this the people rely on the monsoon.

The monsoon is the wet season between May and November, when the rain falls in heavy torrents. If the monsoon fails, the people go hungry. Many people in India have been worried by hunger at some time in their lives.

The monsoon rains can also cause terrible floods in lowland areas such as Bangladesh, making thousands of people homeless and destroying the rice fields.

▲ Washing tame elephants – with some help from the elephants themselves – in a pool in Sri Lanka (which used to be known as Ceylon). This beautiful island is rich in wildlife of all kinds.

▲ The fabulous Taj Mahal, a tomb built by an emperor for his beloved wife more than 350 years ago. Like many of the finest Indian buildings, the tomb itself and the tall minarets are made of delicately carved, cool white marble.

▶ Hindi and English are the official languages in India, but there are over 70 other languages spoken throughout the country. The people love to wear colourful clothes, as you can see from this gathering at Pushkar, a village in northern India.

South-west Asia

▲ The old rubs shoulders with the new in South-west Asia. Most people in the cities now live in blocks of apartments, but here in a remote part of Turkey you can find ancient cave homes, which have been dug out of the soft rock of cliff faces. Some of these caves are still being used as homes today, and you have to climb ladders to reach the doorways.

Lebanon

Israel

Saudi Arabia

◄ Flags sometimes have designs which are an easy clue to the country. The Lebanese flag shows a cedar of Lebanon, a kind of fir tree which once grew wild on the hills here. It is a handsome tree and you often find it planted in parks in Europe and North America. The flag of Israel shows the 'Star of David', who was King of Israel long ago. The flag of Saudi Arabia has Arabic writing. Complicated designs made with this kind of writing are used to decorate the walls and pillars of Muslim religious buildings (such as the Dome of the Rock seen in the picture on the right).

■ Riyadh in Saudi Arabia is the hottest capital city in the world. The temperatures in July rise above 40°C.
■ Saudi Arabia is one of the richest countries in the modern world. It has a quarter of the world's underground oil reserves – but only 14 million people.
■ Turkey has a higher population than any other country in this region. It has 57 million people.
■ Damascus in Syria is the world's oldest capital city.

This region is also called the Middle East. The oil which comes from here provides petrol for Europe – and even for Japan!

It is an area full of contrasts, with rich people and poor people; well-watered fruit orchards and great dry deserts; beautiful coasts and remote mountains; countries at peace and countries fighting wars which never seem to end.

Israel is the Holy Land of the Bible, and places mentioned in the Bible can still be visited today. Jerusalem, the capital of Israel, is the city where both Christianity and Judaism (the Jewish religion) began. The Hebrew language spoken in Israel is the world's oldest language still in use.

But most of the countries here speak Arabic and are Muslim. Mecca in Saudi Arabia has the holiest Muslim shrine and attracts pilgrims from all over the world.

► The traditional head-dress of this Bedouin chief protects his face against the winds and dust of the desert. This head covering can also reveal his rank and the tribe that he belongs to.

Three religions started in this region. Jerusalem is a holy place for Christians, Jews and Muslims. The photograph shows the Dome of the Rock, a Muslim mosque in Jerusalem.

▶ Although giant tankers plough the seas on their way to the oil terminals, quaint old-fashioned craft like these Arabian dhows are still to be seen transporting a variety of goods.

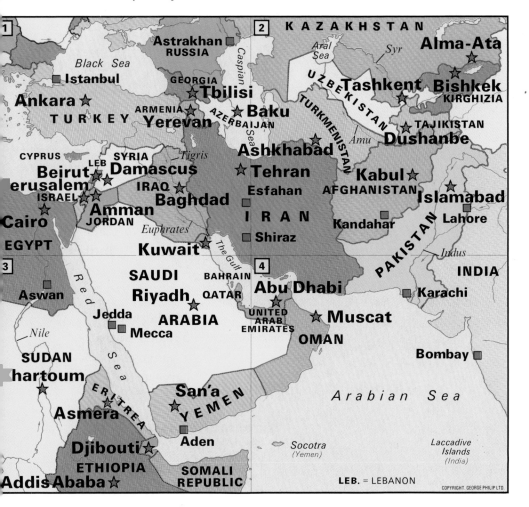

The three continents of Europe, Asia and Africa come together here. It is an old part of the world where Western civilization first began.

Long ago, in the flat valleys watered by the Euphrates and Tigris rivers, the first crops of grain were planted. When the population grew and prospered, they built the first cities here.

In modern times new wealth has come from the oil pumped up from below the desert. Many foreigners come here to work and earn money.

Map information

■ Cities

★ Capital city

Index square–see index

MAP SCALE
This distance is 1400 kilometres

or 700 miles

—— Country boundary

Sea and lakes

River – arrow shows the way it is flowing

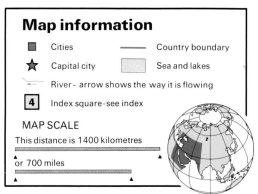

Africa

Area : 30,302,000 square kilometres *(World No.2*
Population : 648 million people *(World No.3)*

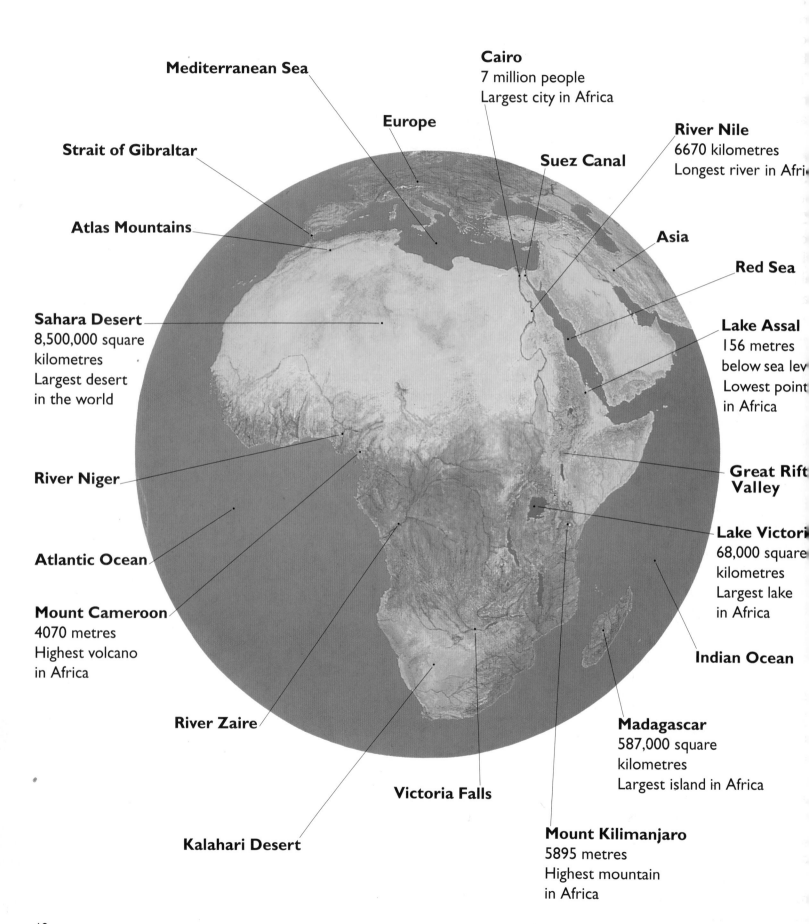

Mediterranean Sea

Cairo
7 million people
Largest city in Africa

Europe

Strait of Gibraltar

Suez Canal

River Nile
6670 kilometres
Longest river in Afri

Atlas Mountains

Asia

Red Sea

Sahara Desert
8,500,000 square
kilometres
Largest desert
in the world

Lake Assal
156 metres
below sea lev
Lowest point
in Africa

River Niger

**Great Rift
Valley**

Atlantic Ocean

Lake Victori
68,000 square
kilometres
Largest lake
in Africa

Mount Cameroon
4070 metres
Highest volcano
in Africa

Indian Ocean

River Zaire

Madagascar
587,000 square
kilometres
Largest island in Africa

Victoria Falls

Kalahari Desert

Mount Kilimanjaro
5895 metres
Highest mountain
in Africa

A typical scene in northern Nigeria. Open country covered with pale grass and dotted with green trees can be seen in many African countries where the land is too high above sea level for jungle to grow. The people here often live in huts in small villages, and each day take their cattle to graze on the grass.

The famous Victoria Falls on the River Zambezi where it forms the boundary between Zambia and Zimbabwe. Large numbers of tourists now visit Africa to see sights like this, and also to see the lions, elephants and other wildlife in the famous game parks.

▼ An oasis in the Sahara Desert in Algeria, with its valuable well. Without the water in the well, the nomads who travel across the desert could not survive. Most of the trees in the picture are date palms. When ripe, the dates are picked and dried in the sun to give a valuable food, full of energy.

Africa is an immense continent (only Asia is bigger). Africa stretches 4000 kilometres on each side of the Equator.

Near the Equator it is tropical with thick jungle where the land is low-lying. But there are also high grassy tablelands and great ranges of mountains.

Some African mountains are so high that they keep a cap of snow all year round. But most of Africa has only two seasons – wet (when it rains) and dry!

North of the tropics stretches the Sahara, the world's largest desert. It occupies a third of the whole of Africa. Another desert lies to the south – the Kalahari.

To reach hidden Africa, the first European explorers followed the rivers inland to the tribal kingdoms.

North and West Africa

NAZik

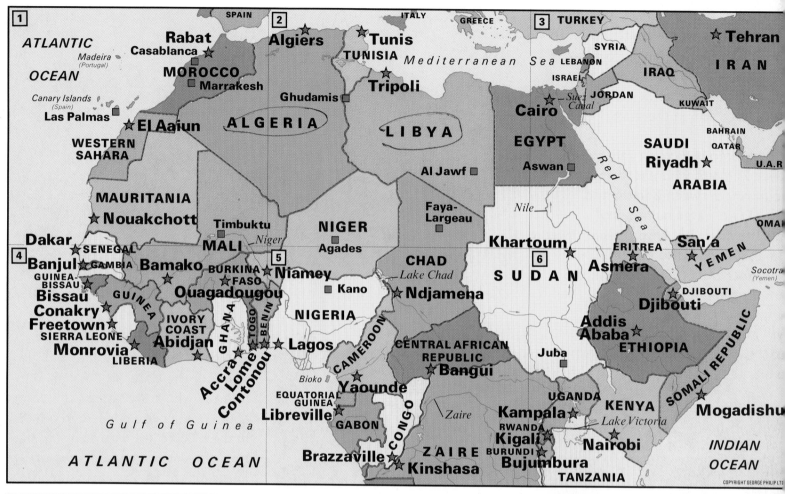

Map information

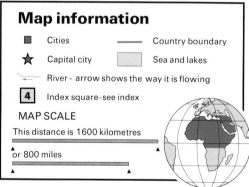

- ■ Cities
- ★ Capital city
- ⌐ River - arrow shows the way it is flowing
- 4 Index square-see index
- — Country boundary
- Sea and lakes

MAP SCALE

This distance is 1600 kilometres

or 800 miles

- ■ After Nigeria, Egypt is the most populated country in Africa with 53 million people.
- ■ The Suez Canal links the Mediterranean with the Red Sea. It is 173 kilometres long.
- ■ Morocco is one of only three kingdoms left in Africa.

Although the countries around the Gulf of Guinea are tropical and wet, water is scarce further north.

Frontiers here run straight where they cross the Sahara Desert. This desert is spreading southwards, and in the Sahel region around Lake Chad the grass and cattle are dying, and the people are hungry.

Long ago, the water of the River Nile made Egypt one of the greatest countries in history. Ethiopia is another old kingdom. It has existed as a country for 2000 years, but drought and war have now made it so poor that 72,000 people must share one doctor.

But for some countries, such as Libya, the discovery of oil has brought wealth in recent years.

Algeria

Ivory Coast

Somali Republic

Egypt

▲ Most of the countries in North Africa are Muslim and their flags often carry Muslim symbols. The Ivory Coast is one exception. It gained its name from the trade in elephant tusks. It was from here and neighbouring lands that slaves were taken to the American plantations.

Tourists come to Egypt to see the yramids and the stone Sphinx that uards them. The Pyramids were the ombs of kings in days gone by.

▶ A tribal chief from Kano in Nigeria sits among his tribesmen who carry ceremonial fans. There are many different tribes in Nigeria.

▲ An elegant 'felucca' sailing on the River Nile north of Aswan. Until the Aswan Dam was built, the River Nile spilled out over its banks each year, not only watering the fields but also making them fertile.

◀ The camel, the 'ship of the desert', can survive a march of many days without water. Even in the modern world of jeeps and helicopters, many desert people still rely on camels to help them cross the sandy wastes.

Southern and East Africa

South Africa

Zaire

Zimbabwe

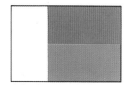

Madagascar

▲ Zimbabwe and Zaire were once European colonies but they are now governed by their own people, and so is the island of Madagascar. South Africa, though, is still ruled by white people. In South Africa the people live in separate areas in the towns and in the countryside according to the colour of their skin.

▲ Mount Kilimanjaro rises steeply over the plains of Tanzania. The snows never melt on its peak.

◄ The lion is just one of many different animals to be seen on a safari holiday here in Zimbabwe. A group of lions is called a 'pride'.

Africa has a magnificent variety of wildlife.

Madagascar has been an island for such a long time that it has its own kinds of animals which are not found anywhere else in the world.

The world's most famous wildlife parks are on the grassy plains of East Africa. Here elephants roam freely and lions hunt among the herds of zebras and antelopes. The animals pay no attention to cars, and visitors can take photographs from the safety of their jeeps.

- Lake Victoria is the largest lake in Africa. It is 68,000 square kilometres in area.
- The longest river in southern Africa is the Zaire (once called the Congo) at 4670 kilometres long.
- Namibia is one of the driest countries in the world.

Africa was once known as the 'Dark Continent', a land of mystery for Europeans until explorers in Queen Victoria's reign revealed its secrets. The discovery of the Victoria Falls on the River Zambezi was a famous milestone in exploration.

Lake Tanganyika, Lake Malawi and other long thin lakes mark the line of the steep-sided Great Rift Valley, which runs for 8700 kilometres down eastern Africa.

In the east there are high open grasslands and also rich farmlands where tea, tobacco and other crops are grown.

To the west the land is lower, hotter and wetter, and there are thick jungles in Zaire. Further south it becomes drier again, and in the south of Botswana there is even a desert – the Kalahari. South Africa has more water, and there is good farmland and many orchards.

Masai girls and children. Their heavy neck ornaments are a sign of the wealth of their families. The Masai are proud nomads who still wander freely with their hump-backed cattle on the great plains near the borders of Kenya and Tanzania. There are 120 different tribes living in Tanzania. Such tribes surprisingly have very little in common with each other, which can often lead to tension and conflict between people.

Map information

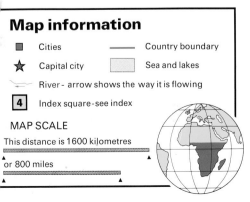

- ■ Cities
- ★ Capital city
- —— Country boundary
- ▭ Sea and lakes
- ⌇ River - arrow shows the way it is flowing
- **4** Index square - see index

MAP SCALE

This distance is 1600 kilometres

or 800 miles

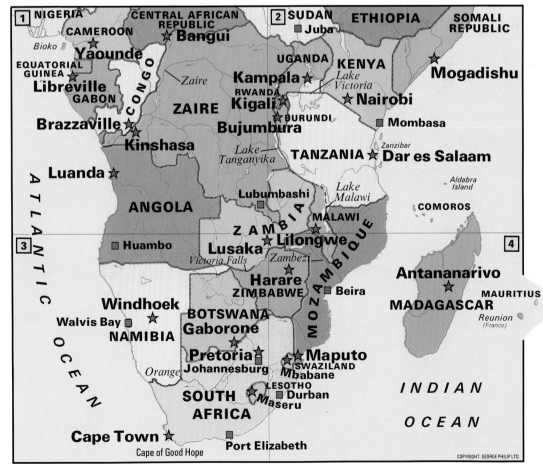

1 NIGERIA
CAMEROON
Bioko
Yaounde ★
EQUATORIAL GUINEA ★
Libreville ★
GABON
Brazzaville ★
Kinshasa ★
CONGO
Luanda ★

CENTRAL AFRICAN REPUBLIC
★ **Bangui**

Zaire
ZAIRE
Kampala ★
RWANDA
Kigali ★
BURUNDI
Bujumbura ★
Lake Tanganyika
TANZANIA

2 SUDAN
■ Juba
UGANDA
Lake Victoria
★ **Nairobi**
KENYA

ETHIOPIA

SOMALI REPUBLIC
★ **Mogadishu**

■ Mombasa
Zanzibar
★ **Dar es Salaam**
Aldabra Island

ANGOLA
Lubumbashi ■
Lake Malawi
COMOROS

ZAMBIA
MALAWI
Lilongwe ★
☐ Huambo
Lusaka ★
Victoria Falls
Zambezi

3 ATLANTIC OCEAN

MOZAMBIQUE
Harare ★
ZIMBABWE ■ Beira

Windhoek ★
Walvis Bay ■
NAMIBIA
Gaborone ★
BOTSWANA
Pretoria ★ ■
Johannesburg ■
Orange
SOUTH AFRICA
LESOTHO
★ Maseru
■ Durban
SWAZILAND
☆ **Maputo**
Mbabane ■

4
Antananarivo ★
MADAGASCAR
MAURITIUS
Reunion (France)

INDIAN OCEAN

Cape Town ★
Cape of Good Hope
■ Port Elizabeth

COPYRIGHT. GEORGE PHILIP LTD.

Australia and Oceania

Area : 8,557,000 square kilometr
(World No.

Population : 26 million people
(World No.

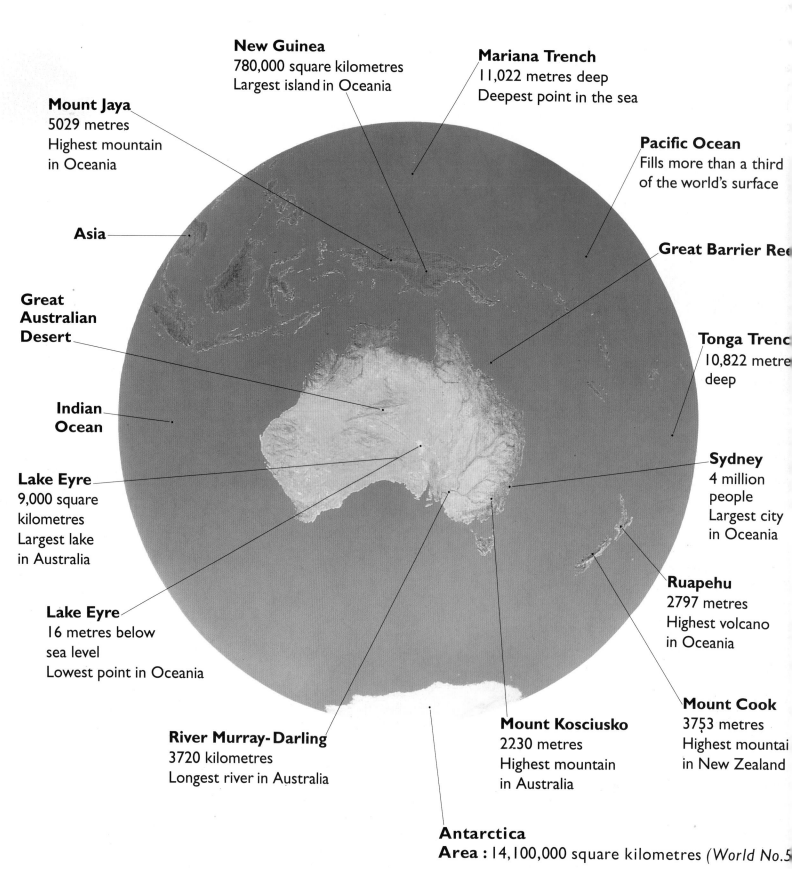

New Guinea
780,000 square kilometres
Largest island in Oceania

Mariana Trench
11,022 metres deep
Deepest point in the sea

Mount Jaya
5029 metres
Highest mountain
in Oceania

Pacific Ocean
Fills more than a third
of the world's surface

Asia

Great Barrier Ree

**Great
Australian
Desert**

Tonga Trenc
10,822 metre
deep

**Indian
Ocean**

Lake Eyre
9,000 square
kilometres
Largest lake
in Australia

Sydney
4 million
people
Largest city
in Oceania

Lake Eyre
16 metres below
sea level
Lowest point in Oceania

Ruapehu
2797 metres
Highest volcano
in Oceania

Mount Cook
3753 metres
Highest mountai
in New Zealand

River Murray-Darling
3720 kilometres
Longest river in Australia

Mount Kosciusko
2230 metres
Highest mountain
in Australia

Antarctica
Area : 14,100,000 square kilometres *(World No.5*

◀ Mysterious stone heads on Easter Island, a small island in the Pacific only 3780 kilometres from the coast of South America. These stone heads were carved hundreds of years ago.

▼ A coral island on the Great Barrier Reef which stretches along the north-east coast of Australia. The deeper water is a dark blue colour; the shallows are paler.

▶ Snowy Mount Cook on South Island, New Zealand. New Zealand is too near Antarctica to be tropical, and parts of it look like the Rockies or the Alps.

▼ The Olgas near Ayers Rock in Northern Territory, Australia, stand in the middle of miles of scrubby desert. In some years little or no rain at all falls here.

The continent of Australia is by far the largest area of land in this part of the world. It has ranges of mountains and great deserts.

Most of this region consists of open ocean and countless islands of every kind. Many are the tops of mountains rising from the deep bed of the sea, while some islands are ringed with coral.

Where it lies across the Equator, this region is tropical, and the ocean also brings great storms. Early sailors made use of its winds and currents to make quicker journeys. They found their way by following the stars.

Australia, New Zealand and the Pacific

This part of the world is often called Australasia, because Australia is the largest area of land. Apart from Australia and New Zealand, the region is mostly open ocean scattered with many coral reefs and islands.

The seas are a barrier to wildlife, and Australia has koala bears, kangaroos and other animals which are found nowhere else in the world.

The first European settlers did not arrive in Australia until only 200 years ago. Today most Australians live along the coasts, leaving the hot barren centre of the country to sheep farmers – and kangaroos! Here the 'flying doctors' have to visit their patients by plane.

Australia

Papua New Guinea

◀ The Australian flag has the Union Jack in one corner because it was once a British colony. It is still part of the Commonwealth. Papua New Guinea's flag shows a bird of paradise.

▲ The unusual white building near the centre of this photograph of Sydney is the Opera House, which overlooks the busy harbour. There are several lovely beaches near the city of Sydney including the famous Bondi Beach, where many people enjoy the sun and the surf.

- Though twice the size of India, Australia has only 16 million people – but 160 million sheep!
- As Australia is in the southern hemisphere, Christmas Dinner can become a summer picnic.

◀ New Zealand has cooler, wetter weather than Australia. In some places it has forests of trees rather like those of Europe or North America. Many of the farms have great flocks of sheep – sheep farming is a major source of income.

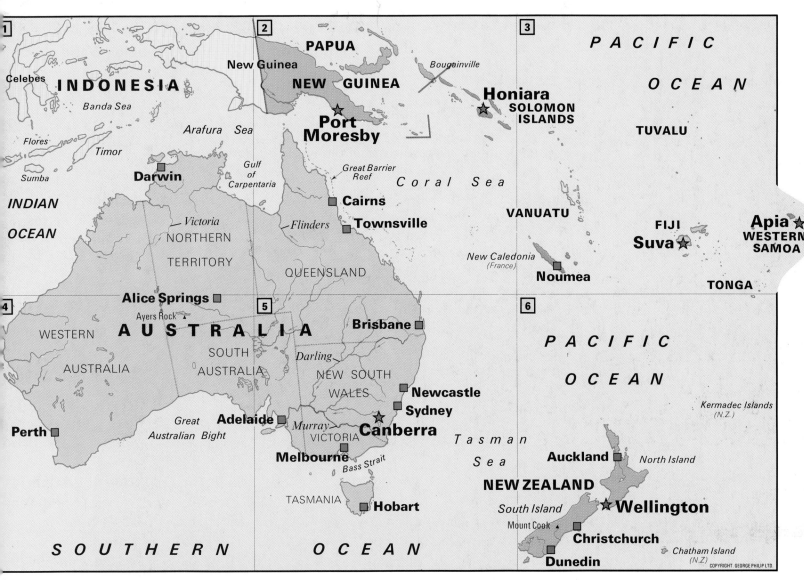

1	**2** PAPUA	**3** P A C I F I C

1 INDONESIA
Celebes
Banda Sea
Flores
Timor
Sumba

INDIAN OCEAN

Darwin

Victoria
NORTHERN
TERRITORY

Alice Springs

Ayers Rock

4 WESTERN
AUSTRALIA

AUSTRALIA
SOUTH
AUSTRALIA

Perth

Great
Australian Bight

2 PAPUA
New Guinea
NEW GUINEA
Bougainville

Port Moresby

Arafura Sea

Gulf of Carpentaria

Great Barrier Reef

Cairns

Flinders

Townsville

QUEENSLAND

5

Brisbane

Darling

NEW SOUTH WALES

Adelaide

Murray

VICTORIA

Melbourne

Newcastle
Sydney
Canberra

Bass Strait

TASMANIA

Hobart

3 P A C I F I C
O C E A N

Honiara
SOLOMON ISLANDS

TUVALU

Coral Sea

VANUATU

FIJI
Suva

Apia
WESTERN SAMOA

New Caledonia (France)
Noumea

TONGA

6 P A C I F I C
O C E A N

Kermadec Islands (N.Z.)

Tasman Sea

Auckland
North Island

NEW ZEALAND

Wellington

South Island
Mount Cook

Christchurch

Dunedin

Chatham Island (N.Z.)

COPYRIGHT. GEORGE PHILIP LTD.

S O U T H E R N   O C E A N

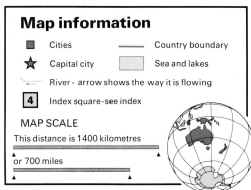

Map information

■ Cities   ── Country boundary

★ Capital city   ▨ Sea and lakes

⌐ River - arrow shows the way it is flowing

4 Index square-see index

MAP SCALE

This distance is 1400 kilometres

or 700 miles

◄ Papua New Guinea lies north of Australia and closer to the Equator. It is tropical, with dense jungle. Old customs are still very much alive and traditional native dances are often seen. The warriors who dance are adorned with colourful feathers taken from the exotic jungle birds. Here the people speak 'pidgin'.

North America

NAZiK

Area : 24,241,000 square kilometres *(World No...)*
Population : 427 million people *(World No.4)*

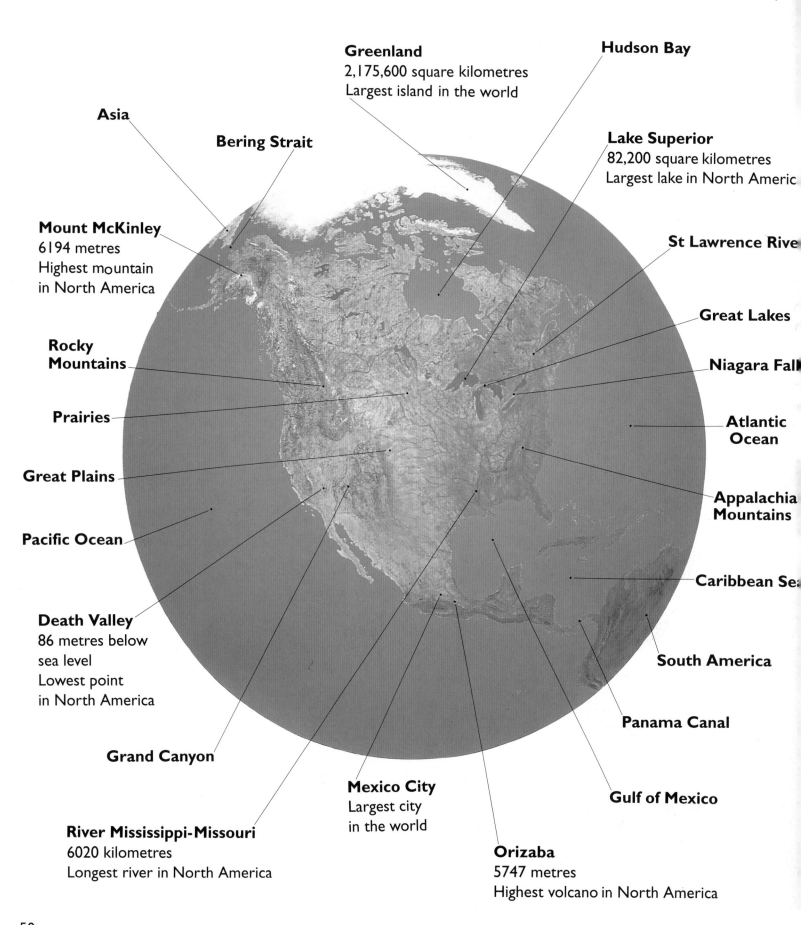

Greenland
2,175,600 square kilometres
Largest island in the world

Hudson Bay

Asia

Bering Strait

Lake Superior
82,200 square kilometres
Largest lake in North Americ...

Mount McKinley
6194 metres
Highest mountain
in North America

St Lawrence Rive...

**Rocky
Mountains**

Great Lakes

Niagara Fall...

Prairies

**Atlantic
Ocean**

Great Plains

**Appalachia...
Mountains**

Pacific Ocean

Caribbean Se...

Death Valley
86 metres below
sea level
Lowest point
in North America

South America

Panama Canal

Grand Canyon

Mexico City
Largest city
in the world

Gulf of Mexico

River Mississippi-Missouri
6020 kilometres
Longest river in North America

Orizaba
5747 metres
Highest volcano in North America

These are the mighty 'Horseshoe' or Canadian Falls, which form part of the Niagara Falls on the Niagara River. They are on the border between Canada and the USA.

A natural stone monument in Monument Valley, Arizona, in the USA. It is called a 'butte'. The rock has been weathered and split by the winds and by the frosts of the desert nights which can be very cold.

The Great Plains of the USA stretch between the Appalachian and Rocky Mountains. They were once unfenced grassy prairies on which herds of wild buffalo roamed, but much of the land is now ploughed for growing wheat. The dry deserts lie towards the west: this is the real cowboy country.

On the west coast, California has some of the best weather in North America, rather like that of the Mediterranean countries in Europe.

In the north, the Arctic spreads its grip over much of Canada. The melting of the winter snows feeds hundreds of lakes.

◀ One of the snowy peaks of the Rocky Mountains in British Columbia, Canada. These high mountains march down the western side of the whole of North America.

Canada

NAZIK

Canada

◄ The maple leaf on the flag is the national emblem of Canada. Its colour is the red that the green leaves become in the season known as the 'fall' in North America (the season known as autumn elsewhere).

■ Canadians speak English, but French is also spoken, especially in Quebec.
■ Forests cover more than half of the total land area of Canada, and it has the most lakes in the world.

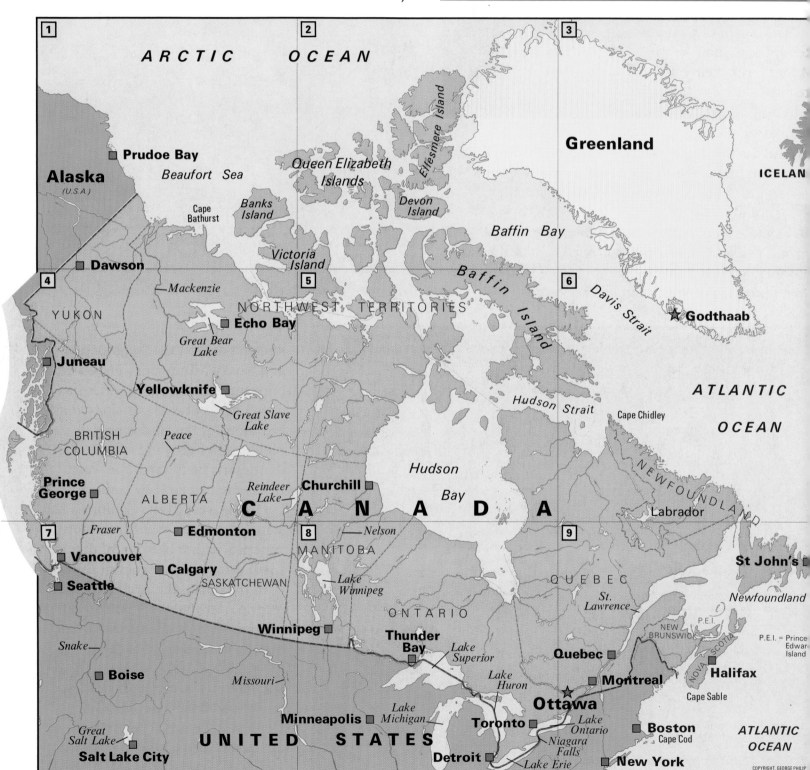

ARCTIC OCEAN

Prudoe Bay
Alaska (U.S.A.)
Beaufort Sea
Cape Bathurst
Banks Island
Queen Elizabeth Islands
Ellesmere Island
Devon Island
Greenland
ICELAN

Dawson
Victoria Island
Baffin Bay

Mackenzie
NORTHWEST TERRITORIES
Baffin Island
Davis Strait
Godthaab

YUKON
Echo Bay
Great Bear Lake

Juneau

Yellowknife
Great Slave Lake
Hudson Strait
Cape Chidley
ATLANTIC OCEAN

BRITISH COLUMBIA
Peace
Hudson Bay

Prince George
ALBERTA
Reindeer Lake
Churchill
NEWFOUNDLAND
Labrador

Fraser
Edmonton
Nelson
MANITOBA

Vancouver
Calgary
SASKATCHEWAN
Lake Winnipeg
QUEBEC
St John's

Seattle
ONTARIO
St. Lawrence
Newfoundland

Snake
Winnipeg
Thunder Bay
Lake Superior
Quebec
P.E.I.
NEW BRUNSWICK
P.E.I. = Prince Edward Island

Boise
Missouri
Lake Huron
Montreal
NOVA SCOTIA
Halifax
Cape Sable

Great Salt Lake
Minneapolis
Lake Michigan
Toronto
Ottawa
Lake Ontario
Boston
Cape Cod
ATLANTIC OCEAN

Salt Lake City
UNITED STATES
Detroit
Niagara Falls
Lake Erie
New York

CANADA

COPYRIGHT. GEORGE PHILIP

the far north, Greenland has
nks with Denmark, while Alaska is
state of the USA.

In between them stretch Canada's
reat Northwest Territories. These
re treeless and very cold. But
rther south thick forests grow
etween many lakes, and there
re open prairies with farms and
rasslands for cattle.

To the west of Canada are the
ocky Mountains and the Coast
lountains. Their valleys fall
eeply to the Pacific Ocean.

Many Canadian rivers have
pids and falls. This means that
ost of the country's electricity
omes from hydroelectric power.

◀ The Calgary Stampede is the largest rodeo in the world. Cowboys can show off their skills, such as wrestling a steer to the ground, or riding a bucking bronco. The rides last seconds rather than minutes!

▲ Huskies running at speed. Dog teams remain popular, although skidoos are now commonly used.

▲ Most Canadians work in modern towns. This is Toronto with the amazing CN Tower, which is one of the world's tallest buildings.

◀ Forests cover half of Canada. The cut logs float to the mills on rivers, and are made into wood pulp and paper to be sold around the world.

Map information

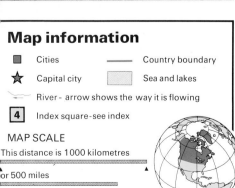

■	Cities	── Country boundary
★	Capital city	Sea and lakes

〜 River - arrow shows the way it is flowing

4 Index square-see index

MAP SCALE

This distance is 1000 kilometres

or 500 miles

United States of America

N.Azik

▲ The Golden Gate Bridge in San Francisco is one of the tallest and longest suspension bridges in the world.

▶ An old-fashioned paddle boat on the Mississippi River. Can you tell how many states this river passes through?

USA

◀ At first there were 13 United States of America, each with a star and a stripe on the flag. Today there are 50 states with a star, but they must all share the 13 stripes!

The USA holds many records:
■ Disney World in Florida is the world's largest theme park.

■ Lake Superior is the world's largest freshwater lake – 82,200 square kilometres.

A few American Indians retain their old traditions, but the families of more than three-quarters of today's Americans came as settlers from Europe, starting with the Pilgrim Fathers in 1620.

Other Americans are descended from the slaves brought from Africa to work on the cotton plantations in the southern states. Slavery was ended in 1865, when the northern 'Yankee' states won a civil war fought against the south.

After the Civil War, the states forgot their quarrels and in time made the USA the richest and most powerful nation in the world. The White House with the President's office is in Washington, but the state capitals still remain very important today.

◀ The 'Clothes Peg Tree' is a tall redwood tree in a forest near Yosemite National Park in California. It is shaped just like a clothes peg.

1 ■ Seattle
WASHINGTON

■ Portland
OREGON

Snake

MONTANA

NORTH DAKOTA

2 C A N A D A
■ Winnipeg

MINNESOTA

St. Lawrence

3

Lake Superior

Lake Huron

■ Quebec

■ Montreal
MAINE

■ Halifax

IDAHO

WYOMING

SOUTH DAKOTA

■ Minneapolis
WISCONSIN

Lake Michigan

☆ Ottawa

■ Toronto

Lake Ontario N.H.

MASS ■ Boston
Cape Cod

Great Salt Lake

NEVADA

■ Salt Lake City

UTAH

Missouri

NEBRASKA

IOWA

■ Chicago

Detroit ■

ILLINOIS INDIANA OHIO

Lake Erie

■ Cincinnati

NEW YORK
PENNSYLVANIA NEW JERSEY

■ New York

CONN R.I.

☆ Washington

■ San Francisco

CALIFORNIA

■ Las Vegas

Colorado

COLORADO

■ Denver

KANSAS

■ Kansas City

■ St. Louis

WEST VIRGINIA

D.C.
DELAWARE MARYLAND

4 U N I T E D   S T A T E S

5

Arkansas

MISSOURI

Ohio

KENTUCKY

VIRGINIA

6

■ Norfolk

os Angeles

ARIZONA

NEW MEXICO

■ Amarillo
OKLAHOMA

ARKANSAS

TENNESSEE

NORTH CAROLINA

CONN. = Connecticut
D.C. = District of Columbia
MASS. = Massachusetts
N.H. = New Hampshire
R.I. = Rhode Island
VER. = Vermont

■ Phoenix

Red

Mississippi

SOUTH CAROLINA

■ Charleston

Gulf of California

Lower California

■ Ciudad Juarez

TEXAS

■ Dallas

LOUISIANA

MISSISSIPPI

ALABAMA GEORGIA

■ Atlanta

ATLANTIC

PACIFIC

Rio Grande

■ Houston

■ New Orleans

FLORIDA

Cape Canaveral

OCEAN

OCEAN

MEXICO

■ Monterrey

Gulf of Mexico

BAHAMAS

■ Miami

Cape Sable

☆ Nassau

Alaska and Hawaii are also states.

COPYRIGHT. GEORGE PHILIP LTD.

Map information

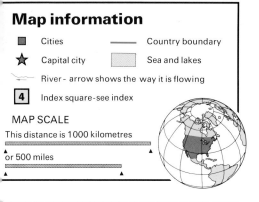

■ Cities

★ Capital city

━ River - arrow shows the way it is flowing

4 Index square - see index

─── Country boundary

▨ Sea and lakes

MAP SCALE

This distance is 1000 kilometres

or 500 miles

■ The busiest roads in the world are the 'freeways' of Los Angeles.
■ The largest living thing in the world is a giant redwood tree in California, 83 metres high and probably 3500 years old.
■ Death Valley, California, is one of the hottest places in the world: in 1917 the temperature here stayed above 48°C for 43 days!

Two hundred years ago, the 13 states on the east coast of America broke their links with Europe and joined together as a new nation.

Settlers then went west in covered wagons, creating new states in the new lands that they found. Today there are 50 states in the USA, and they include Alaska (which is attached to Canada) and Hawaii far out in the Pacific Ocean.

The north-eastern states are crowded and industrialized, while the mid-west states have prairies and open farmlands.

In the far west are the Rocky Mountains and deserts – these states are famous for cattle rearing.

▶ Before air travel became common, settlers from Europe arrived in the USA by ship, passing the Statue of Liberty on their way into New York.

Central America

▲ A macaw parrot from the jungle of Costa Rica. The jungle here is a haven for wildlife.

▲ A candlestick cactus in a desert i Mexico. In some years no rain at all falls on these deserts.

Map information

- ■ Cities
- ★ Capital city
- ── Country boundary
- ▨ Sea and lakes
- River - arrow shows the way it is flowing
- 4 Index square-see index

MAP SCALE

This distance is 1200 kilometres

or 600 miles

■ With 18 million people, Mexico City is the largest city in the world. It is still growing!

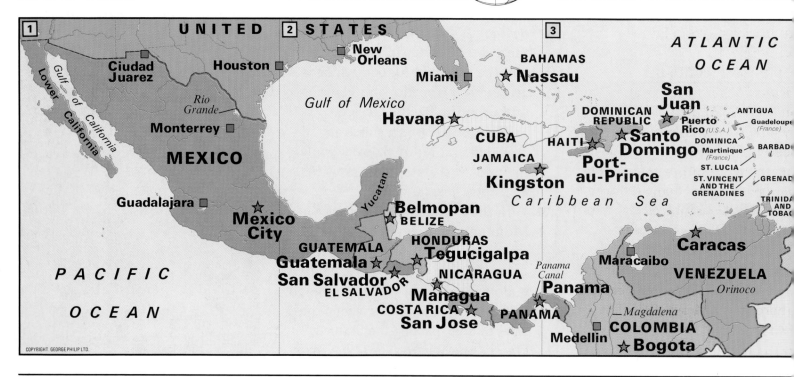

UNITED STATES

ATLANTIC OCEAN

Ciudad Juarez

Houston

New Orleans

Miami

BAHAMAS

★ Nassau

Rio Grande

Gulf of Mexico

Havana ★

CUBA

DOMINICAN REPUBLIC

San Juan

★ Puerto Rico (U.S.A.)

ANTIGUA

Guadeloupe (France)

Monterrey

HAITI ★ Santo Domingo

DOMINICA

Martinique (France)

BARBAD

MEXICO

JAMAICA

Port-au-Prince

ST. LUCIA

ST. VINCENT AND THE GRENADINES

GRENAD

Guadalajara

Kingston

Caribbean Sea

TRINIDA AND TOBA

Yucatan

Belmopan

★ Mexico City

★ BELIZE

GUATEMALA

HONDURAS

Tegucigalpa

Caracas

Maracaibo

Gulf of California

Lower California

Guatemala ★

San Salvador ★

EL SALVADOR

NICARAGUA

Managua ★

Panama Canal

Panama

VENEZUELA

Orinoco

PACIFIC OCEAN

COSTA RICA ★

San Jose

PANAMA

Magdalena

Medellin

COLOMBIA

★ Bogota

◄ This stone temple is in a clearing of the Mexican jungle. It was built by the Mayan civilization over 1000 years ago.

The islands in the Caribbean are also known as the West Indies. They vary in size and character – some are large and mountainous, others have farms and banana plantations, while many are small flat coral islands with coconut palms behind long sandy beaches.

Many different people live on the islands. Some speak Spanish, others English. But they all share the violent hurricanes that often occur in this region. The hurricanes cause a lot of damage and can even uproot the trees.

Central America stretches like a thin bridge of land strung between the two vast continents of North and South America.

It is very varied, however, and in some places there are mountains and deserts, in others dense jungles or rich farmland. Coffee plants were first grown in Costa Rica and today bananas and other jungle fruits are grown in farms in many countries.

Central America has a long history. Some of today's cities are built on ancient ones. Cities built by long-forgotten nations have also been found hidden in the thick jungle. Some of the countries here were part of the Spanish empire and Spanish is still the main language in many of them.

Mexico

Panama

Jamaica

Puerto Rico

◄ These countries are independent, but does the flag of Puerto Rico remind you of the flag of a great country not very far away? Although they speak Spanish and their country lies 1600 kilometres to the south, the people of Puerto Rico are citizens of the United States of America. However, they cannot vote in American elections unless they live in the USA itself.

A ship entering a lock on the Panama Canal. Opened in 1914, it provides a quick journey between the Atlantic and Pacific Oceans. Up to 15,000 ships use it each year.

South America

Area : 17,793,000 square kilometres *(World No.4*
Population : 297 million people *(World No.5)*

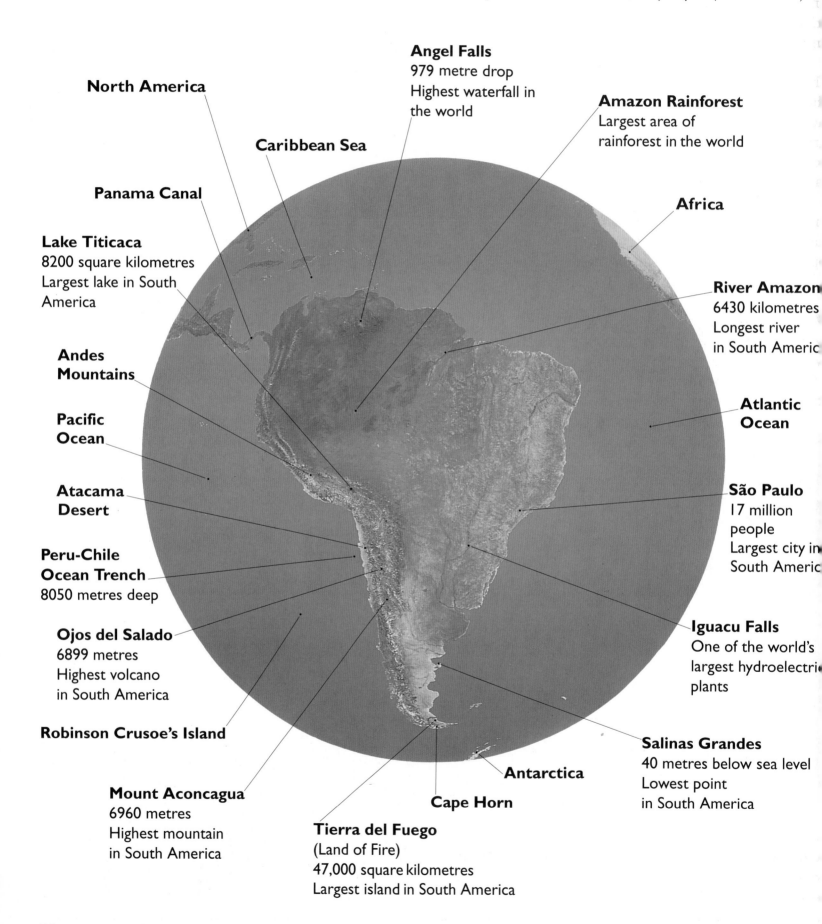

Angel Falls
979 metre drop
Highest waterfall in
the world

North America

Amazon Rainforest
Largest area of
rainforest in the world

Caribbean Sea

Africa

Panama Canal

Lake Titicaca
8200 square kilometres
Largest lake in South
America

River Amazon
6430 kilometres
Longest river
in South Americ

**Andes
Mountains**

**Atlantic
Ocean**

**Pacific
Ocean**

**Atacama
Desert**

São Paulo
17 million
people
Largest city in
South Americ

**Peru-Chile
Ocean Trench**
8050 metres deep

Ojos del Salado
6899 metres
Highest volcano
in South America

Iguacu Falls
One of the world's
largest hydroelectri
plants

Robinson Crusoe's Island

Salinas Grandes
40 metres below sea level
Lowest point
in South America

Antarctica

Mount Aconcagua
6960 metres
Highest mountain
in South America

Cape Horn

Tierra del Fuego
(Land of Fire)
47,000 square kilometres
Largest island in South America

When Europeans first landed in America, they thought it was India, and the name 'Indian' for native tribes has stuck. There are many Indian tribes in South America.

The Andes are a great mountain chain. The lowlands are tropical in the north and there are vast jungles here. Further south there are open grassy plains and even deserts in some places, and very cold empty lands near Cape Horn.

Although there is some industry and mining, and some countries have large ranching and farming operations, South America is mainly a continent of poor people.

▼ This is Machu Picchu in Peru. It was the refuge of the Incas, who were defeated by the Spanish in the 16th century. It stood ruined and forgotten for hundreds of years.

▲ The River Amazon snakes its way for 6430 kilometres from its source in the Andes. For much of the time this river flows through trackless 'rainforest'. Large areas of this jungle are still unexplored.

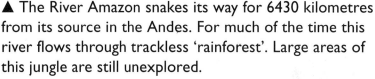

▶ A village on the shores of Lake Titicaca high in the Andes. Life here is simple but harsh. Everything that the countryside has to offer is used. The boat is made from reeds which grow beside the lake.

South America

Brazil

Argentina

Chile

Venezuela

◄ These countries were once colonies of Spain and Portugal, although their flags do not show any similarity to the European ones. Spanish is the main language of them all except for Brazil, where it is Portuguese. However, there are also many native Indian languages which are still spoken. 'Quechua' is spoken in Bolivia and northern Chile.

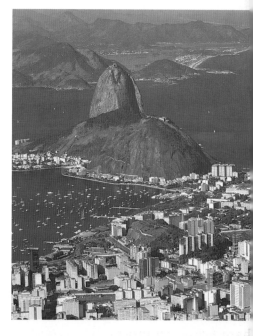

▲ Llamas in Bolivia with coats of thick warm wool to protect them from the bitter cold. They can carry heavy loads over the dangerous paths of the high Andes.

► Sugar Loaf Mountain enhances the splendour of Rio de Janeiro.

▼ Tribesmen in the Amazon jungle still hunt with traditional weapons.

This continent stretches like a vast triangle pointing from the tropics to Antarctica, from the damp sweaty heat of the Equator to the cold of Cape Horn. On either side of the River Amazon stretches the largest tropical jungle in the world. It is still not completely explored.

The Andes run for 7200 kilometres down the west side, forming the longest mountain chain in the world. They are also very high, and Bolivia and other mountainous countries have air which is so thin that visitors must rest sad take things very gently for the first few days.

Local women wait patiently in a market near Lake Titicaca, which lies 3811 metres above sea level.

The motto of many countries in South America could be 'riches but no money'. Even in those countries which have reserves of oil, metals or fertile soils, the wealth is not fairly shared out and most of the people remain poor.

But many of the countries here in South America are lively places. Brazil is famous for its samba dancing, which is seen each year at the famous street carnival in Rio de Janeiro.

Map information

■	Cities	——	Country boundary
★	Capital city		Sea and lakes

River - arrow shows the way it is flowing

4 Index square-see index

MAP SCALE

This distance is 1400 kilometres

or 700 miles

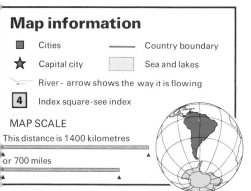

- Mount Aconcagua is the highest mountain in South America. It is in Argentina.

- La Paz, Bolivia, is the highest capital city in the world. It is 3627 metres above sea level.

Polar Regions

The Arctic consists of a thick layer of ice which spreads as far as the coast of Greenland. The Arctic Circle is an imaginary line, north of which the Sun does not set at all on midsummer's day.

By contrast, Antarctica has ranges of mountains deeply covered by snow and ice. Here the weather is the worst in the world. Blizzards are very common.

- The South Pole was first reached in 1911, two years after the North Pole.
- Antarctica is 14,100,000 square kilometres in area.

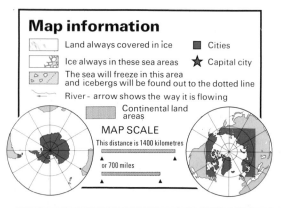

▲ Ships carrying supplies often have to break through the ice.

Map information

Land always covered in ice	Cities
Ice always in these sea areas	★ Capital city

The sea will freeze in this area and icebergs will be found out to the dotted line

River - arrow shows the way it is flowing

Continental land areas

MAP SCALE

This distance is 1400 kilometres

or 700 miles

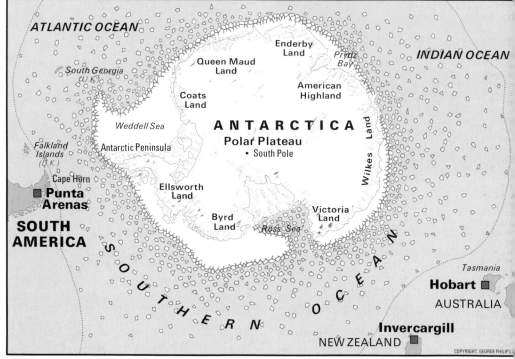

ATLANTIC OCEAN

INDIAN OCEAN

South Georgia (U.K.)

Enderby Land

Prydz Bay

Queen Maud Land

American Highland

Coats Land

Weddell Sea

ANTARCTICA
Polar Plateau
• South Pole

Falkland Islands (U.K.)

Antarctic Peninsula

Cape Horn

■ Punta Arenas

SOUTH AMERICA

Ellsworth Land

Byrd Land

Victoria Land

Wilkes Land

Ross Sea

SOUTHERN OCEAN

Tasmania

Hobart ■
AUSTRALIA

Invercargill

NEW ZEALAND ■

COPYRIGHT. GEORGE PHILIP L

▼ Although penguins cannot fly, they are good swimmers in the icy seas off Antarctica.

PACIFIC OCEAN

Siberia

Lena

ASIA

Yenisey

■ Anchorage

Alaska

New Siberian Islands

Yukon

Beaufort Sea

Severnaya Zemlya

RUSSIA

Ob

Mackenzie

ARCTIC OCEAN
North Pole •

NORTH AMERICA

Queen Elizabeth Islands

Svalbard

Barents Sea

Archangel ■

★ Moscow

■ Churchill

Baffin Island

Greenland

Scandinavia

EUROPE

CANADA

Godthaab ★

★ Reykjavik

Iceland

Cape Farewell

British Isles

ATLANTIC OCEAN

COPYRIGHT. GEORGE PHILIP LTD.

Index

This is a list of the names that are on the maps. They are in alphabetical order. All the names beginning with A are first and then B and so on to Z. After the name there are two numbers. The first one is the page number and the second the map square where you will find the name. If the name goes over from one map square to another, then the square given in this list is the one where the name begins.

There are also maps on the endpapers, that is, on the inside of the front cover and back cover. The Equator line divides these maps into top and bottom, and the centre of the book into right and left. In the index *Hawaiian Islands* **flt** means you will find the name on the front endpaper, on the left side and the top half; **b** = back or bottom, **t** = top, **f** = front, **l** = left and **r** = right.

PHOTOGRAPHIC ACKNOWLEDGEMENTS

AA Photolibrary p. 12 (tr)

B. & C. Alexander p. 53 (t)

J. Allan Cash Photolibrary pp. 18 (tl), 21 (tl), 24 (t), 27 (t & b), 29 (tl), 35 (b), 36, 37 (c), 38 (b), 39 (tr), 41 (t & c), 43 (tl), 44 (t), 47 (b), 48 (t), 51 (tl & tr), 54 (tl & tr), 55, 56 (tl & tr), 59 (bl & br), 60 (tl)

Julian Baum & David Angus/Science Photo Library pp. 6-7 (also used on pp. 8, 28, 40, 46, 50, 58)

Britstock-IFA p. 16; **Britstock-IFA**/Stadelmann p. 19; **Britstock-IFA**/Bernd Ducke pp. 32 (t), 59 (t); **Britstock-IFA**/Ben Simmons p. 32 (b); **Britstock-IFA**/Raj Kamal p. 45

Finnish Tourist Board p. 11 (tr)

Susan Griggs Agency/Adam Woolfitt p. 23 (tl)

Robert Harding Picture Library pp. 12 (tl), 14, 15 (tl), 17 (tl & tr), 18 (tr), 21 (c & b), 24 (b), 26, 27 (c), 29 (tr), 35 (tl), 43 (br), 47 (cr), 48 (b), 51 (b), 53 (bc), 54 (b), 57 (t & b), 62 (b)

The Hutchison Library pp. 9 (b), 21(tr), 29 (b), 31 (c), 32 (c), 33, 34, 37 (t), 44 (b), 47 (t & cl), 60 (tr), 61

Magnum Photos/Nick Nichols p. 60 (b)

Planet Earth Pictures/Peter Stevenson p. 35 (tr); **Planet Earth Pictures**/Nicholas Tapp p. 49

Russia Photolibrary/Mark Wadlow pp. 30, 31 (t)

Charles Swithinbank p. 62 (t)

Zefa Picture Library pp. 5, 9 (t & c), 10, 11 (tl & b), 12 (b), 5 (tr & b), 17 (b), 18 (b), 23 (tr & b), 24 (c), 31 (b), 37 (b), 38 (t), 39 (tl), 41 (b), 43 (tr & bl), 53 (bl & br)

t – top; c – centre; b – bottom; tl – top left; tc – top centre; tr – top right; cl – centre left; cr – centre right; bl – bottom left; bc – bottom centre; br – bottom right

Mountains, Rivers and Seas

ARCTIC

Greenland

Bering Strait

Yukon

Alaska
▲ Mount McKinley

Aleutian Trench ▾   Aleutian Islands

Mackenzie

Victoria Island

Ellesmere Island

Baffin Island

Hudson Bay

Britis Isles

ROCKY Mountains

NORTH

AMERICA

Missouri

Great Lakes

St. Lawrence

Newfoundland

Azores

Mississippi

Bermuda

Canary Islands

Hawaiian Islands

Sierra Madre

Gulf of Mexico

Milwaukee Deep ▾

ATLANTIC

West Indies

Cape Verde Islands

PACIFIC

Caribbean Sea

CENTRAL AMERICA

OCEAN

Palmyra Islands

Kiritimati

Equator

Galapagos Islands

OCEAN

Amazon

Andes

SOUTH

Ascensie

Phoenix Islands

Kiribati

Tokelau Islands

Samoa

Society Islands

Marquesas Islands

Tahiti

Tuamotu Archipelago

AMERICA

St. Hele

Tonga

▾ Tonga Trench

Tubuai Islands

Pitcairn Islands

Parana

Easter Islands

Kermadec Islands

Kemadec Trench ▾

Aconcagua

Tristan da Cunha

Andes

Chatham Islands

Falkland Islands

South Georgia

Cape Horn

SO

Antarctic Peninsula